The School Governors' Yearbook

2019

21st edition

Adamson Publishing

The editor is indebted to all the authors named at the end of their articles and to David Marriott for his helpful comments on the proofs.

Copyright © 2018 Adamson Publishing Ltd

Published by Adamson Publishing Ltd
info@adamsonbooks.com
www.adamsonbooks.com

ISBN 978-0948543-64-7

British Library Cataloguing in Publication Data
A catalogue record for this book is available from the British Library

Cover design by Geoff Shirley
Cover photo from iStockphoto

Printed by Ashford Colour Press Ltd

Preface

A recent report published by the Institute of Education Press at University College London (Greeny and Higham, *Hierarchy, Markets and Networks: Analysing the "self-improving school-led system" agenda in England and the implications for schools*) says that the accountability regime has had an undue influence on schools. It more than counterbalances the autonomy that has been extended to them, with the result that they are effectively being steered by the state from the centre. "Making sure my school does well in Ofsted" is a top priority for the majority of headteachers. Yet autonomy and local initiative are supposedly at the heart of our educational system; moreover, they also underpin our system of governance. Indeed, if the governor's job is just to ensure that our schools comply with central prescription, what point, apart from saving the state money, is there is in making unpaid volunteers responsible for them?

Nevertheless, in practice governors are far from lackeys of the state and do have a lot of power, even if they are not always aware of how much. But now it is time to exercise more of it. They know their schools and pupils far better than any external authority so they should use their powers in the way that they think best, irrespective of strictures of the accountability regime. As we argue in the following pages, various familiar features of our schools show the current importance of this. The "system" of schooling that has evolved is in fact incoherent and marooned in a half-finished state. More creativity is desperately needed in the curriculum, but the arts are being tightly squeezed. The way school leaders are trained is inadequate for the jobs they are expected to do. The workload pressures on staff are driving skilled teachers out of the profession, while the pressures on children have led to an alarming rise in the incidence of child mental health problems.

Some of these problems may seem far too big for governors to tackle. But in the words of an old slogan, to change things you should think global but act local. Governors should start by considering the needs of the children in their own schools and decide whether getting the right grades in English and maths or passing the Ebacc are in fact the top priorities for all of them. This means not just thinking about the short term, but looking ahead and preparing them for a complex and ever changing world. And not least, making them confident and well-balanced individuals. Moreover, this cannot be done without considering the needs of the adults who work with them and develop them. The tools are there in governors' hands. What governors need is the courage to take risks, to challenge orthodoxy, and adhere to their principles. The majority of governors have these qualities or they would not have been motivated to volunteer for the role. We hope that this book will help you assert them.

STEPHEN ADAMSON, Editor

Contents

part one RECENT CHANGES AND CURRENT ISSUES

part two PLANNING AND RESOURCES

part one

Recent Changes
and Current Issues

2019

The year that was

September 2017
✳ The Secretary of State for Education, Justine Greening, announces that compulsory Key Stage 1 tests (SATS) are to be abolished in 2023.
✳ A revised National Funding Formula for schools is published.

October
✳ Resolution Foundation claims that Universal Credit threatens the existence of free school meals. Currently they are triggered by working tax credit, which is being abolished with no comparable replacement.
✳ Sir Theodore Agnew replaces Lord Nash as under secretary of state for the schools system, with responsibility for school governance.
✳ DfE figures for 2015–16 show a 40 percent increase in the number of permanent exclusions over four years.

December
✳ Ofsted's annual report reveals that 89 percent of schools are good or outstanding.
✳ Government launches plan for children suffering from anxiety and depression to receive counselling in their schools.
✳ Concern arises at the growing number of failing academies, whose original sponsor has been removed without a new one being found. DfE figures show 64 schools, containing over 40,000 pupils, are in this position.

January 2018
✳ The *TES* reports that the total number of school governors has reduced by about a quarter in a few years, to 250,000, attributing the decline to the growth of multi-academy trusts.
✳ The *Observer* newspaper reports that six of the ten largest academy trusts have raised concerns about funding pressures.
✳ The DfE publishes new national performance tables, which give comparative performances of multi-academy trusts, at both Key Stage 2 and Key Stage 4.
✳ Mayor of London announces that the capital's schools will be sent alerts when air pollution in their area rises to hazardous levels.
✳ Widespread publicity is accorded to the collapse of Carillion, whose portfolio of activities includes providing meals, cleaning and caretaking services to schools, and which also sponsors an academy.
✳ Headteacher in Newham bans girls eight and below from wearing the hijab in school, but is forced by parental pressure to back down, despite receiving the support of Amanda Spielman, head of Ofsted.
✳ Justine Greening sacked as Secretary of State for Education and replaced by Damian Hinds.

February

✱ The exam board OCR finds that over 2000 teachers in a three year period have helped children to cheat in exams they have set. According to the board, the "improper assistance" is rarely seriously punished.

✱ A new Advanced Maths Premium is introduced to incentivise schools to encourage pupils to take maths A and AS levels. The money will be paid to schools for each extra pupil who takes the qualification.

March

✱ Research is published that shows that some of the most pronounced gender pay gaps in the country are in academy chains, in part because of the payment of large salaries to mainly male senior executives.

✱ DfE data shows unauthorised pupil absence at its highest ever level, due to children being taken out for family holidays. 16.9 percent of pupils missed at least half a day of lessons in 2016–17 for a holiday.

✱ Survey by ClientEarth finds 60 percent of parents in favour of traffic being barred from proximity to school gates at the beginning and end of the school day.

April

✱ Support for pupils with SEN is declining under financial and other pressures, according to 62 percent of the teachers surveyed by the teacher union NASUWT.

May

✱ 100 leading artists write to the press condemning the exclusion of the arts from the EBacc measure.

✱ The NAHT reports a 5 percent shift in pupil numbers from mainstream to specialist provision between 2010 and 2017.

✱ The Secretary of State for Education, Damian Hinds, tells the National Association of Headteachers that accountability measures will be simplified, with floor standards and coasting combined in a single measure.

✱ Report finds that white students are twice as likely as black ones to be admitted to Oxford.

June

✱ Survey of year 11 pupils by the DfE finds that the incidence of bullying has declined over 10 years, but that girls are now more likely to be bullied than boys, especially over social media.

✱ Damian Hinds tells the NGA's summer conference that the amount of money to be spent by the DfE on governor training will double, to £6 million, by 2021.

July

✱ A report confirms that a grammar school in Orpington had been forcing out pupils it considered would not get good A level grades.

What a state we're in

The educational landscape in which governors operate has never seemed more complex and the direction of travel more uncertain.

For any governor who has lived through the last few decades in education, the present can seem as unfamiliar as the pre-National Curriculum state of education, because we have become used (if not inured) to constant turmoil.

Post-1988, especially, education became – to use a hackneyed phrase – a political football, as each new Secretary of State sought to make an instant impact by introducing more changes and initiatives than schools had time to implement properly. Over a period of 20 years there were no fewer than 19 Education Acts, most long forgotten. School leaders and governors learned how to ignore the most hare-brained policies, or at least neuter them by implementing the absolute minimum of what was required, while getting on with the real and important business of running the school.

The Coalition Government assumed power in 2010 and Education Secretary Gove launched his White Paper *The Importance of Teaching* within a couple of months of taking office, leading to the Academies Act – arguably the last really significant education legislation to date. We governors are still living with its many consequences – not all of them good.

In 2016, we saw the implementation of the Education and Adoption Act, which essentially tightened up some of the nuts and bolts of the Academies Act. And that's it. The current government made clear in the first Queen's Speech after the general election that it has no intention of proposing any new education law this parliament.

Prior to that there had been half-hearted attempts to establish a way forward, including Nicky Morgan's White Paper *Education Excellence Everywhere*, whose over-excited plans to induce mass academisation and wipe out parent governors were sunk within a few weeks of publication. Only the Fair Funding proposals survived. Theresa May's – sorry, Nick Timothy's … er, sorry again, Justine Greening's Consultation Paper on the reintroduction of grammar schools fell at the first hurdle of the snap election.

It seems that they have simply thrown in the towel. And how strange the world of education feels now. No new policy initiatives. No fantasy projects based on the Education Secretary's misremembered school days. No unfunded projects designed to create a world class education system within a matter of months.

It's like a night scene from an old cowboy movie when the twitchy cowpunchers sense that all is not right: "It's quiet, Hank … too damned quiet."

For years schools and their governors have pleaded in vain for time to consolidate and implement previous policies before the next tranche is "rolled out", to no avail. In response, we were told that change is the only constant and we simply had to accept that and get on with it. But now there's a hiatus, school leaders don't seem to be welcoming the breathing space with open arms. There is no obvious reason for this, unless they are too shocked by the novelty of the situation to make good use of it. Perhaps they would like to take advantage of it but do not trust the silence to last. Or perhaps they are just too tired ...

A half-finished project

And as we look around the eerily quiet educational landscape, what do we see?

A half-finished project, with no realistic prospect of completion. A monument to short-termism, lack of attention to detail or consideration of the consequences, intended and unintended. A mess of competing interests and systems. A frightening loss of teachers and heads with no sign of a turnaround. A terrifying sense of an underfunded educational estate where widespread bankruptcy looms.

One missed advantage of the political interference model is that at least someone in authority seemed to be paying attention even if they didn't fully grasp how the system actually worked and what it really needed in order to prosper. Now no-one has their eye on the ball, at a national level. It's hard to remember the name of the latest secretary of state let alone say what his policies might be, because he does not appear to have any.

There are turf wars between Ofsted and the Regional School Commissioners, which have required the Secretary of State to promise intervention. The DfE appears to be interested only in academies and MATs, which make up just about one third of all schools in the country. The National College for Teaching and Leadership is being disbanded. The House of Commons Education Committee (amongst many other well-informed canaries in the coalmine) regularly warns of the many flaws in the system, based on extensive research, only to be comprehensively ignored.

The academies juggernaut seems to be shuddering slowly to a halt now that any governors wanting to take on academy status for their school have already done so and those that have not have yet to be convinced of any good reason to change. The imaginary army of disgruntled and/or idealistic teachers, parents and others who were supposedly itching to establish new free schools have vanished into the ether so that only existing academies now set them up. Academies that formed small, local MATs are being pressurised to double or treble in size in order to become economical. Some large MATs have fallen apart, spectacularly. There is a small but growing number of SNOWs (Schools that Nobody Wants) rejected by sponsor academies and no longer on the local authority's books – a model of what might be the future for many more schools. Local authorities are pale shadows of what they once were, in most cases, lumbered with legal obligations they can barely meet because they no can no longer afford to employ staff or provide resources. One authority has already gone bust.

So what about the 66 percent of schools that are not academies? As local services and support mechanisms dwindle away, they are in real danger of becoming isolated and increasingly non-viable. Teaching unions and heads' associations continue to raise the alarm but their voices are ignored, if heard. Dioceses have taken the strain in many cases but largely for faith schools, of course. And their resources are finite.

Governors are urged to ensure their schools have strategic plans in place, but where is the national long-term strategic plan for education?

The academies movement has gone too far for it to be dismantled but not far enough for it to be the default model. "Move fast and break things" was Facebook's mantra and it clearly worked, up to a point. Disruption is dramatic and relatively easy. Breaking an existing system can be achieved because there is something to take apart. What happens once it's gone, though? If you carry on breaking things, eventually there's nothing left to smash but you have to keep moving fast in order to escape any accountability. The architects of this unholy mess are long gone to other government departments or other organisations like Leave.EU and will never have to face the consequences of their egotism and folly.

Where does this leave governors?

Is there a way forward? Governors have few options but to focus on their own school and do their best to mitigate the effects of the unholy mess on teachers, children and families. "Splendid isolation", however, carries many risks in such an uncertain time. Collaboration with local schools (other than through MATs) remains possible and perhaps the best way to go, even if it may be informal and limited to increasing our collective buying power.

Back at the chalk face, day by day, schools get on with the routine job of educating children. It used to be easy to assume that this would continue, whatever the latest government's education policy was. Now it seems less certain, since academy trusts can implode, debts outrun income and support services disappear. And no-one in government seems interested in education nor has any viable plan to deal with the growing crisis in our education system. Time to take back control?

DAVID MARRIOTT

A broad and balanced curriculum?

Governors are in a position to resist the narrowing of the curriculum, but it requires standing up to an outdated orthodoxy.

In 1939, in a famous (at least amongst educationalists) book called *The Sabre-Tooth Curriculum* H.R.W. Benjamin neatly illustrated the classic tension between a modern curriculum based on mastering the skills needed to prosper in contemporary life and one that celebrated more traditional and less utilitarian values. In his fable, pre-Ice Age society taught children three main subjects: fish grabbing with the bare hands, woolly horse clubbing and sabre tooth tiger-scaring with fire. As a new Ice Age dawned and technology improved, these skills became redundant. New skills were demanded by a changed environment: fishnet making and using, antelope snare construction and operation, and bear catching and killing.

In Benjamin's fable, those proposing this new curriculum were met with opposition: "The school curriculum is too crowded now... What we need to do is to give our young people a more thorough grounding in the fundamentals. Even the graduates of the secondary schools don't know the art of fish grabbing in any complete sense nowadays, they swing their horse clubs awkwardly too, and as for the old science of tiger scaring – well, even the teachers seem to lack the real flair for the subject which we oldsters got in our teens and never forgot... If you had any education yourself you would know that the essence of true education is timelessness... You must know that there are some eternal verities, and the sabre tooth curriculum is one of them!"

As his book points up, in the long history of education what's in the curriculum and how much time each subject deserves has been a philosophical, political and cultural battleground. The National Curriculum that emerged in 1988 (after some bloody skirmishes between the advocates of competing subjects) was designed to settle the matter, but then it started to be nibbled away at by subsequent Secretaries of State for Education of differing political persuasions.

Is the curriculum living in the past?

Since 2002 schools and governors have had a legal obligation to ensure that the school curriculum be balanced and broadly based, and "should promote the spiritual, moral, cultural, mental and physical development of pupils at the school and of society and prepare pupils at the school for the opportunities, responsibilities and experiences of later life".

Despite the various changes to the National Curriculum since it was introduced – streamlined, less prescriptive and not even compulsory in the 33 percent of the nation's schools that are academies – the statutory obligation on governors to ensure breadth and balance remains.

Much more recently Amanda Spielman, Her Majesty's Chief Inspector of Schools, has suggested that this aim is not being met: "Young people get one opportunity to learn in school and we owe it to them make sure they all get an education that is broad, rich and deep... One of the areas that I think we sometimes lose sight of is the real substance of education. Not the exam grades or the progress scores, important though they are, but instead the real meat of what is taught in our schools and colleges: the curriculum."

Undoubtedly, the national focus in recent years has been dominated by literacy and numeracy, which was kick-started by the Blair government's literacy and numeracy hours and continues to this day – reinforced by Ofsted inspections, some would argue. There are, of course, compelling justifications for this, since children's progress in many other subjects depends on mastering the basics. But it has, along with an increasingly rigorous and relentless testing regime, led to severe challenges to the notion of breadth and balance in the curriculum. The Ebacc at secondary level forces schools to value core subjects more highly than others, while financial restraints can limit staff training, materials and resources, which have a knock-on effect on the subjects on offer. This is sometimes compounded by staff shortages, particularly in some specialist subjects at secondary level.

It is often argued that there is a correlation between the narrowing of the curriculum and a remorseless assessment culture and the worrying growth of mental health issues among young people. Some parents boycott SATs tests in order to protect their children from the worst effects of this.

As evidence, governors may have noticed one or more of the following behaviours in their schools:

- class time given over to SATs practice papers before Christmas in Year 6
- neglect of those areas of the Key Stage 2 curriculum that are not examined in order to concentrate solely on those areas that are: stopping art, DT, music and other subjects during SATs year
- starting GCSEs in Year 9 (or earlier)
- squeezing out arts subjects in Key Stage 4 to allow for ever greater English and maths allocations
- using GCSE specifications as a model for designing the Key Stage 3 curriculum
- teaching to the test.

These are all indicators of a possible restriction of the fullest curriculum. All are understandable, since schools are still judged largely by what can be measured easily and the consequences of failure are draconian.

Governors are placed in a difficult position, then, charged with protecting a rich and deep curriculum but also with, in Lord Nash's words from the *Governance Handbook*, "tackling underperformance, challenging mediocrity, and setting the highest of expectations; refusing to accept second best for any child". When "underperformance" is measured by narrow metrics in just two subjects, this worthy aim can become unduly restrictive.

The classic defence of the value of a broad and balanced curriculum is that it enhances performance in literacy and numeracy by keeping children interested in education in and for itself, creating opportunities for children to succeed in one or more of many subjects. Literacy and numeracy can be further developed through most other curriculum subjects. Early engagement in music, drama and sport has helped to produce some of the best known and most successful people in our society, not all of whom excelled in literacy and numeracy. Enriching the curriculum through a variety of extra-curricular activities can help children struggling with the basics retain an interest in school and extend the knowledge and understanding of the majority.

Keeping the curriculum in focus

Linking governors to subjects was, and still is, in some cases a way of helping governors understand the breadth of the curriculum and champion "Cinderella" subjects, though there seems to be a trend away from this model. With or without these links, governors should ask regularly for reports on the humanities, DT, science, PE and arts subjects to ensure that the school does not lessen its focus on them. Inviting specialist teachers to give short presentations about their subjects to governors can also keep them in the spotlight.

We should, as a matter of course, ensure we are familiar with:

- the rationale for the organisation and delivery of the curriculum
- the evaluation of the impact of the curriculum
- the effectiveness of professional development to support teachers in delivering a broad and balanced curriculum
- how well pupils are prepared for key points of transition
- the impact of the curriculum on pupils' spiritual, moral, social and cultural development, mental and physical health and well being.

We should also ask ourselves, from time to time:

- How does the curriculum relate to our vision and values?
- Is there something we have not included in our curriculum that we consider important or interesting?
- Is the curriculum we're offering the one we'd want our own children to experience?

And, ultimately, in the context of the sabre-tooth curriculum fable, are we preparing children for the future or the past?

DAVID MARRIOTT

Tackling teacher overload

It is vitally important to schools to be able to recruit and retain quality teachers. However, problems relating to the retention of teachers and the link to unreasonable workload have continued to make headlines.

Teacher recruitment and retention were a major area of concern at the annual teacher union conferences in the spring, as was widely reported in the national press. Surveys by the NEU and NASUWT both showed that large numbers of respondents had considered leaving the teaching profession due to workload pressures (81 percent and 65 percent respectively). Governors and senior leaders are reporting that it is becoming increasingly challenging to fill teaching vacancies.

The problem is not new and the Department for Education (DfE) set up workload challenge review groups to try to address it in 2014. Three independent reports were published as a result, on marking policy, planning and teaching resources, and data management (see the 2016 Yearbook). The latest *Governance Handbook* states that governing boards should have regard to the principles and recommendations in these three reports, and governors are urged to use them to review their current policies and practices with the aim of easing the burden on teachers.

Not long after he was appointed Secretary of State for Education, Damian Hinds further addressed the problem of teacher workload. He has focused on two key areas: the constant change and new national initiatives that bring with them additional planning, and the burden on teachers created by Ofsted accountability. For his part he has made a commitment to giving schools a minimum lead-in time for significant changes in policy in accountability, curriculum and qualifications. In addition, Ofsted has clarified its requirements about inspection in order to reduce unnecessary workloads in schools, which are now contained in paragraph 28 of the school inspection handbook. The DfE website has a video, pamphlet and posters (www.gov.uk/government/publications/teacher-workload-poster-and-pamphlet) offering tips on workload management and a *Workload Reduction Toolkit*, published in July 2018. There have also been revised staffing advice and a guide to flexible working.

Addressing the issues at school level

The welfare of teachers and the workload pressures have to be a concern for governors. There are various steps they can take, in their strategic role, to support schools in addressing the issue.

1. Ask senior leaders questions about teacher workload. What is the working culture like in school? Does the school know the views of staff when it comes to workload? Are workload questions included

in regular staff surveys? Is the school aware of and making use of the latest materials and the findings of the three independent reports?

2. Look at staff turnover and recruitment. Do governors monitor staff turnover figures over time? Are staff offered exit interviews and do senior leaders report on the key reasons for staff leaving?

3. Follow up on the three reports. Has the school reviewed its marking, lesson planning and data collection policies in light of the DfE independent reports? Do senior leaders know how long their staff spend working outside the classroom? Can they demonstrate that the time outside the classroom is having an impact on pupils' learning?

4. Consider governors' own expectations. Have governors thought about their own demands on staff time? Do governors review and consider the work-life balance of their school leader? Do governors ask for data to be presented in a special way? Do governors expect lengthy reports? Is there a simpler way of giving governors the information they need?

5. Ask what the school leadership is doing about staff wellbeing. Do senior leaders consider and promote staff wellbeing? How are staff supported with managing their workloads? Are there models of good practice in promoting wellbeing that the school could learn from? Has the school considered the new advice on flexible working? Are workload and wellbeing included in the performance management policy?

The most recent DfE survey on the topic, in 2016, suggests that teachers are still working an average of 54.4 hours a week. It is encouraging to see that the DfE is considering the impact national policy changes and the perceived demands of Ofsted have on the working life of teachers, and it is refreshing to think that teachers are being encouraged to focus on the interaction they have with children and young people in the classroom, where studies clearly show they make the most difference in terms of pupils' learning. But the challenge still rests with governors to ensure that their schools are doing what they can to ensure that teachers enjoy their jobs and stay and flourish in the profession.

SIAN MATHIAS

Talking points: being political

Most of us keep our politics separate from governance work, whatever our beliefs. But can you do this and fulfil your role of getting the best for your pupils? For example, we have many educational disparities in this country – notably on socio-economic, ethnic or gender lines. But there is also a geographical one. According to the chair of the Education Select Committee a "stark educational gap" exists between the North of England and other parts of the country. The roots of this are in decades of policies and attitudes that have prioritised economic development in the South over the North. You cannot tackle that just by working in your school.

Using your data sources

Understanding data, and knowing the range that is available, is an essential element of governance, but it also comes with caveats.

Nothing seems easier to collect today than data. Schools are no exception. Not only do they generate a lot of it for their own uses, but there are other organisations that do much of the work of organising and interpreting raw data for them. Data also forms the basis of inspection, as no Ofsted inspector will set foot in a school without having looked at its key performance figures.

Governors also need key data, at a certain level. As they are expected to hold the leadership team to account for the school's performance, the choice is to gather their own data on how pupils are doing or to access it from elsewhere. Fortunately, they do not need to undergo the impossible because what they need is readily available from some reliable sources.

The essential measures, by which the school is judged by others, are the results in end-of-phase tests and exams: Key Stage 2 SATs in primary schools, GCSE and other public exams in secondary schools, and A level and AS level results in sixth forms. For each, governors need:

- overall results for pupils as a whole
- the ability to look at individual groups of pupils (boys, girls, pupils eligible for the Pupil Premium, pupils with SEND, etc)
- a means of evaluating the data
- pupil progress against some defined starting point
- ready availability.

How the data is presented is also important. Most governors are not statisticians and require data that is organised in a way that is easy to understand and analyse.

There are three forms of data available that do this, though they vary in how well they meet each of these criteria.

Analyse School Performance

The government does much of the work. It takes SATs and exam results from all schools, and publishes school league tables that measure the performance of schools against each other. The information is also made available to each school and its trustees/governors through Analyse School Performance: an online document of just a few pages. Primary schools are given the percentage of pupils achieving the expected standard (measured as 100 in the SATs) in each of reading, writing and maths, and those achieving a higher standard in the same subjects, measured as 110 or more. "Expected standard" and "higher standard" are based on pupils' prior attainment. A further means of judging what this means is given by setting the school's figures against national and local averages. The report also contains the results in Key Stage 1 tests, in phonics, and for Early Years.

Secondary school results are given for pupil performance in GCSEs by those achieving grade 4 and above (the "expected standard") and 5 and above (a "higher standard"). Results are also given for a suite of eight subjects for both attainment (Attainment 8) and Progress (Progress 8), and the number achieving the Ebacc. Progress 8 is particularly significant as it records how pupils have progressed across secondary school, irrespective of their starting level.

ASP provides segmented analysis. You click on "view pupil breakdown" to see the data for separate pupil groups, and there is a separate tab for showing the results for disadvantaged pupils. The information is presented in scatterplots with circles (for disadvantaged pupils) and squares (for non disadvantaged ones) representing individual pupils so that you get a sense of how pupil performance clusters. The version of ASP produced for governors does not identify pupils by name, but a separate version for teachers does. The scatterplots enable you to see how much a few very high or very low performers might affect the overall averages. Colour coding for averages makes it easy to use.

Ofsted's data summary report

What ASP does not provide is figures on a school's performance historically. These are instead available in Ofsted's Inspection Data Summary Report (IDSR), which is accessed by clicking on "Reports" on ASP. IDSR is intended primarily for inspectors to read before visiting a school, but is also useful to governors, particularly those awaiting an inspection. It has much more data than the ASP, some of which the average governor would not particularly need to know, but a record of key data over a three year period adds an important dimension. Although it can be a mistake to read too much into comparison of one year against the next, as no two cohorts will be identical in ability, the comparison enables you to assess the school's progress, not just overall but in individual subjects.

IDSR also sets the school in context. You may be broadly familiar with the number of pupils for whom English is an additional language, those with SEND, or those eligible for the Pupil Premium, but it helps assess the school's performance if you have the hard figures in relation to national and local norms.

Finally, one aspect of IDSR that all governors should know is not simply statistical at all. This is Areas to Investigate, which identifies the school's main strength and weaknesses. Also, to help interpret the report, Ofsted publishes *Guidance for the Inspection Data Summary Report* (https://assets.publishing.service.gov.uk/government/uploads/system/uploads/attachment_data/file/700596/General_guidance_for_IDSRs_v4.pdf).

ASP, with its link to IDSR, is accessed online through a DfE portal, Sign-in, via a password that your school should give you.

Fischer Family Trust

The data used by Ofsted forms the basis of the Fischer Family Trust School Dashboard for Governors. As the title says, this eight-page report for each school is produced specifically for governors, on FFT Aspire. One problem with all data reports, even those that are pared down, is sorting out what really matters from what does not. The FFT report colour-codes data for significance, showing where, for example, a pupil group is too small for much to be read into the statistics. As in the IDSR, attainment and progress are given over three years, and there are breakdowns of the headline results by pupil groups. Unlike the IDSR, all GCSE subjects are recorded in the version produced for secondary schools. The data is given in a very visual way, using colours and with dashboards relating KS2 and KS4 attainment and progress to national averages. FFT also scores by publishing reports based on unvalidated data in September for primary schools and the beginning of November for secondaries, several weeks before the corresponding reports from the DfE and Ofsted.

The FFT provides online training on the use of data reports for governors, in a course that takes about an hour.

Unlike the other reports FFT Aspire is not free, but only available to schools that subscribe to the FFT Aspire service.

Sean Harford, Ofsted's National Director of Education, has warned that it is only "meaningful data" that is important, and that what is meaningful varies from school to school. Having data coded to indicate statistical significance is a start, but with 68 percent of schools now judged to be good, what is good should be accepted as the norm and what most governors need to concentrate on is where performance or progress vary appreciably, whether above or below.

Ofsted inspectors only treat data as a starting point, and will want to see and discuss the school in operation. Data is only the starting point for governors too and should be seen as a guide to the school's performance, not the last word. There are always other significant issues: children may achieve well at Key Stage 2 but be emotionally ill-equipped to move on to secondary school; pupils may manage perfectly decent results in English and maths GCSEs but at the cost of developing the subjects that will enable them to excel later in their working lives; the school may be producing much improved results but at a financial cost that means that future pupils are paying for the exam success of the present ones. Statisticians rightly warn us against concentrating on outliers, but that is only when assessing trends. Governors should still seek to know that a good education is being provided for children like the one who was far below the others on the scatterplots. It's a little used phrase now, but it is still true that every child matters.

STEPHEN ADAMSON

Developing your head's strategic competencies

School autonomy means developing leadership that has the skills and initiative to manage change. These have to be found outside of the normal training sources, and require governors to look at the big picture.

A key part of the governors' role is strategic planning, which means preparing a school for an uncertain future. To do this successfully includes ensuring your head has the right skills to lead strategic change, or recruiting a new skillset if required.

Governors recruiting new heads often do so with a particular strategic need in mind, although looking for individuals with very specific competencies is like searching for a needle in a haystack. The training for school leadership does not tend to build strategic capability, such as would be achieved by exposure to case studies or scenario-based challenges, so those candidates who have not yet sharpened their teeth through experience will be lacking in this respect.

This is a critical deficit. It's a given that there will be less money, attention and direction from the centre, so it will be up to schools themselves to lead improvement in the system, taking the initiative to solve problems like teacher retention or system-organisation, without approval from "above". This sort of self-determination in schools and between schools will require people who can lead change, not just cope with it.

Organisation development

There are several forms of professional development around that focus entirely on helping leaders of organisations lead change. For schools, the key ones involve organisation development

Organisation development (OD) is about planned or emergent change, and how to lead it. Its aim is to increase effectiveness and health in an organisation through planned, systematic intervention in its processes and practices. The process is managed from the top and informed by the behavioural sciences. Leaders who understand OD principles will have a better appreciation of how their school functions as an organisation, and how it is likely to respond to change. Moreover, they will understand how its ability to accomplish tasks (or not) and cope with change (or not) depend entirely on how its internal workings are organised, and how they interact.

In this respect, OD – and leadership more broadly – depends on an ability to view an organisation as a system, and to understand thereby how it works: how it functions as an organism. Systems thinking involves critically analysing the relationships between parts in order to develop an understanding that enables better decision-making about the whole. A systems-thinking leader does this in order to make decisions about what is wrong, what to change, and how to manage the impact of that change in a way that achieves an intended effect. This is fundamentally different from a decision-making process in which one changes a part of a complex system, but then might wonder why the whole doesn't change as one wants. Systems thinking also encourages people to understand how their organisation interacts with its external environment, making them less likely to allow it to be a passive victim of externally driven change.

Managing people

So OD is about taking control. It involves a diagnostic phase, which would seek to identify what is really going on in a school, and how its parts – its students, teachers, technologies, structures, etc – might respond in concert to change. Consequently, it also involves organisational behaviour: the psychology of people in the workplace.

This is a very broad and dynamic field, which features at the core of many leadership programmes but not at all in the official ones such as NPQH (National Professional Qualification for Headship) and NPQEL (National Professional Qualification for Executive Leadership). But if you need your school leader to sort out a staffing issue or to lead an overworked team through a complex change (which you do!), they are far more likely to be successful if they have a grounding in OD. For your school is nothing more than the interactions between the people who spend their time in it: the motivations of individuals, the dynamics of groups, and the psychodynamics of the organisation itself. And these interactions have been studied, analysed, and tested by academics and active researchers for many years, resulting in a very broad range of evidence on which your leader can base their practice.

Finally, OD is also about strategic planning. But the old ways, which try to predict and control the future, no longer cut it in an environment characterised by turbulence, uncertainty, novelty and ambiguity (TUNA). The best one can do now is to approach strategic planning as a process of reframing the organisation for a number of possible future scenarios, and adapting as the environment changes. For a number of reasons, this is particularly challenging in the schools' context, but if there's any one particular type of organisation that needs to get its collective head around it, it's schools. Given that your be-all and end-all is about equipping the next generation to live in those unpredictable contexts, you really need your leaders to be on top of this.

Many organisations provide training in OD or aspects of it. This usually means looking beyond the usual providers of school CPD – for example, at the CIPD, Henley Business School, or Roffey Park. The Open University, University College London and Cranfield have introductory courses.

BEN GIBBS

Inspection changes

We are enjoying a period of stability in the framework for the inspection of schools, but there have still been changes that governors need to ensure they know about.

Ofsted has promised that no major changes will be made to the inspection regime before 2019, a pledge that they have repeated for the last couple of years. However, that does not mean that all aspects of the timetables and criteria for inspection have been set in stone for the time being. For example, new versions of the Inspection Handbook for both section 5 and section 8 inspections were issued in April 2018 to take account of amendments to procedure. What it does mean is that what is inspected in schools and the nature of the judgements remain the same.

Those April changes were to re-inspections and short inspections:

- Schools that receive a judgement of requires improvement (RI) for the first time no longer receive a monitoring visit. After a successive second or third RI judgement, schools will continue to be monitored, 12 to 24 months after publication of the report.
- The usual timeframe within which good schools receive a short inspection has been extended from approximately three to four years. The maximum period in which Ofsted will return remains the statutory five years from the end of the academic year of the previous inspection.
- The re-inspection window for schools judged to require improvement, to have serious weakness or being put in special measures can now be as long as 30 months in all cases. Previously the maxima were 30, 18, and 24 months, respectively.

The rationale for the timetable relaxations is to give regional directors greater discretion about the date of re-inspection, allowing them to reflect the circumstances and progress of the schools in question. This fits in with the trend to make inspections less rigid. (However, the increase in time before re-inspection could leave schools vulnerable to losing staff and pupils.) Another recent product of this trend is the removal of the requirement for inspectors to look at performance management procedure, especially the scrutiny of anonymised teacher performance management reports, which was announced in March 2018. The timetable flexibility may also reflect on the cost pressures on Ofsted, which like so much government has experienced budget cuts (the envelope provided by the Department for Education for school inspection is 52 percent less, in real terms, than it was in 2000).

A significant change that was also introduced in early 2018 slipped under the radar. Maintained schools judged three times in a row to require improvement will no longer be automatically subject to an academy order; only a judgement of inadequate can now do that.

Short inspections

The most important change to the manner of inspections concerns schools previously deemed to be good. At the start of 2018 – before the lengthening of the period between inspections was announced – the procedure for converting short inspections was overhauled.

Inspectors continue to convert short inspections, usually within 48 hours, if they have serious concerns about safeguarding or behaviour, or if they think the quality of education provided by a school has declined to inadequate.

When there are no significant issues with safeguarding or behaviour, but inspectors identify potential concerns about either the quality of education or leadership and management, the inspection will not convert. Instead, Ofsted now publishes a letter setting out the school's strengths and areas for improvement. A full inspection then takes place later, typically within one to two years. This will give the school time to address any weaknesses and seek support from appropriate bodies. In the meantime, the letter will be clear that the school's current overall effectiveness judgement has not changed.

When inspectors have reason to believe that a school may be improving towards an outstanding judgement, Ofsted publishes a letter confirming that the school is still good and setting out its strengths and priorities for further improvement. A section 5 inspection then takes place within one to two years, giving the school time to consolidate its strong practice.

Schools that have rated themselves outstanding may be unhappy about having to wait up to two years to have their judgement corroborated. Ofsted will therefore consider requests from schools for early inspections.

From comments that have been made publicly by the HMCI, Amanda Spielman, when revisions are made to the framework, they are likely to be radical. For one thing, it looks as if much more attention will be paid to the curriculum. Be prepared for very different handbooks in September 2019.

STEPHEN ADAMSON

Talking points: home-schooling

Figures obtained by the BBC show a 41 percent rise in three years in the number of children being home-schooled in the UK. Should you worry if children from your own school are taken out to be educated at home? Whereas there will always be some children who are just not school shaped, surely the loss of the social element and of the ability to learn from other children, as well as the benefits to be gained from interacting with a wide range of skilled adults, suggests that home-schooling must be considered an inferior option for the vast majority, and that to opt for it suggests that something is going wrong.

Your data protection responsibilities

The GDPR is now in place, and it leaves governing boards with some extra, ongoing responsibilities that need monitoring.

Many schools, along with all sorts of public bodies, charities and commercial organisations, found themselves working hard in spring 2018 to secure compliance with the General Data Protection Regulations (GDPR) before they came into force. However, just because you managed to do everything then that had to be done, it does not mean that the GDPR can pass into history and receive a big tick as job done. The regulations are about how you handle the constant stream of data that comes into the organisation, plus the treatment of the always growing amount of data that you have acquired in the past.

The governing board holds ultimate responsibility for the school's correct use of personal data, and it is therefore up to it to ensure that the school's procedures are correct, robust and being properly applied. The importance of protecting people's data should have been rammed home by the Cambridge Analytica/Facebook saga, but if that were not enough, organisations that fail in their duties could be subject to massive fines.

Revisiting implementation

Now the dust has settled, this is a good time to revisit the core requirements of the GDPR and check that the school has implemented them:

- that it has appointed a data protection officer (DPO) and that staff know who the person is and are fully appraised of their role
- that staff have been trained in data protection
- that a privacy notice or statement has been issued and parents, staff, pupils and other relevant people have been informed where they can see it, and that it is clear and intelligible
- that the school complies with any subject access requests, or is equipped to do so, within one month of receipt and does not charge a fee
- that policies have been revised as needed.

Schools have the right to share DPOs and many may have done this, especially in MATs. If this is the case for you, it is even more important to ensure staff – and governors – know who they are and what they do, and that the DPO has been inducted into your own school and its context. The DPO must report to the highest level of management, which will be the trust or the governing board, but this can in practical terms mean the headteacher or chief executive, providing that they do not fill the role themselves (not recommended, but not forbidden).

Having a good DPO does not remove the need for other staff to be familiar with the GDPR. All staff, especially teachers and those in the school office, will handle pupil data. They should have had training in data protection. This may well have been given to staff as part of the school's GDPR preparation, but it also applies to staff appointed since then, so check that data protection training is part of induction. It is important that staff know the school's procedures, and also how they should react should, for example, someone claiming to be a police officer contact them with an urgent request for a pupil's contact details. In an emergency the staff member may not be able to contact the DPO to ask for advice, especially if that person does not work in the school.

One of the key principles of the GDPR is that individuals have a right to know what information is held about them, how it is used, and how they can ask for its removal. All affected therefore need to know the school's policy on requesting and holding data, and know whom to contact for information about themselves, both of which should stated in the privacy notice. Needless to say, governors should also be familiar with the privacy policy and be satisfied with it. Information should not be held indefinitely, and indeed the longer it is held the greater chance of its misuse. Ensure that the school has a policy on retention, which includes a requirement that data is not kept beyond its retention date. Expired data must be destroyed securely, in a way that it prevents reconstruction.

Most of the data processing that a school carries out does not need consent, but an important area that does is taking photos of children. This will have been covered already in relation to external publication, but you should make sure that the consent form also covers internal use such as posting photographs on notice boards or displays.

Most of the data held by the school will be legitimate under the "legal task" or "public task" bases for holding information, but some uses will depend on consent. Pupils over 13 can give consent themselves for use of their data for "information society services" (usually a service over the internet). Governors should ask whether the consent forms are clear and simple, and whether it is explained why the data processing is necessary, what will happen to it, and how and when it will be disposed of.

Governors and clerks

All schools, including academies, are obliged by law to hold a data protection policy. As this has been a long-held statutory requirement, it is possible that the policy has not been revised for some time. Or it may have been revised early in the GDPR compliance process, in which case it is unlikely to refer to the Data Protection Act 2018, which replaced the Data Protection Act 1998. This Act only received royal assent on 23 May 2018, two days before the implementation date of the GDPR. Check that your policy is up to date. You may need also to check any policies that cross-refer to it, especially the freedom of information policy, but possibly also health and safety, safeguarding, pupil discipline, special educational needs or whistle blowing.

Your clerk will hold data about the members of the governing board, and, if also required to clerk appeals and exclusions, will be given sensitive information that should not be stored on their personal computer afterwards. If the clerk is a school employee, they will not be a data controller, as that function, with its legal obligations, is held by the school. But if they are under a third–party contract, then they will be a data controller in their own right and liable for the data they handle. (Any contracted organisation with which the school shares data should be required to show that it is compliant with the GDPR.) The Information Commissioners Office says that in such cases the clerk and school should have a contract that:

- ensures that they both understand their obligations, responsibilities and liabilities
- helps them to comply with the GDPR
- helps controllers to demonstrate their compliance with the GDPR
- may increase data subjects' confidence in the handling of their personal data.

The NGA publishes guidance on Clerks and GDPR.

Your security, and that of the information that you exchange around the governing board, is increased by having school email addresses for all on the board. Clerks not using school email addresses should ensure that if they email documents to several governors at once, such as meeting agendas, the recipients are "blind copied" so that their addresses are not accessible should the email be forwarded.

Any breaches in the safe handling of data are potentially serious, and the governing board should receive reports on these. Breaches that cause risk to people's rights and freedoms have to be reported to the Information Commissioners' Office. Governors should want to explore why the breach occurred and to remedy any faults in the school's procedures or training.

How should governors monitor data protection? Staff training, the role of the DPO, implementation of data subject requests and any breaches should be included in the headteacher's report. If aspects of the handling of data cause concern that governors feel need further exploration, there is a temptation to make the whole area of data protection a specific responsibility for one of the board's members. However, even though data protection is important, it is not one of the key governor functions, and should not need this level of involvement. It is, however, an aspect of safeguarding, so can be placed in the remit of the safeguarding link governor.

HARRIET MANSON

Drawing up a scheme of delegation

A published scheme of delegation is not just a requirement in order to be transparent, but a very useful tool to achieve efficiency.

Negotiated and reviewed annually, the scheme of delegation for a school, academy or multi-academy trust (MAT) sets out clearly the responsibilities and extent of the authority delegated by the board to committees, working parties or individuals acting within the framework of the policies formulated by the trust or governing board. It clarifies who is responsible for what – especially in relation to the head and the governors. It should help avoid misconceptions, duplication, misinterpretations and confusion about roles and responsibilities, and should promote better understanding of the way the school or MAT works, together with a more effective use of the people involved. It also demonstrates to Ofsted inspectors how the governing board organises its work.

The problems caused by an ineffective or non-existent scheme of delegation were noted in a letter from ex-Ofsted Chief Inspector Sir Michael Wilshaw to then Secretary of State for Education Nicky Morgan. In some ineffective MATs, he said, there was "confusion over governance structures, reflected in the lack of clarity around the roles and responsibilities of the central trust and the local governing boards [LGBs] of constituent academies. This is not helped by some trusts failing to meet the requirement to publish a scheme of delegation."

The DfE's *Governance Handbook* includes useful guidance on schemes of delegation (in section 5.6), especially in MATs, where the organisation can be more complex than in a single school or academy. As the Handbook says, "all boards have a choice about how they are constituted and organised. Effective boards think carefully about this and in particular about whether and how to use their powers to delegate functions and decisions to committees or individuals."

There are many model schemes available on the internet and it makes sense to work from an existing version rather than a blank sheet of paper, as long as the model chosen is relevant to the kind of school yours is. The National Governance Association's models are a good place to start.

Here are some steps you could take towards writing or reviewing your scheme:

- Read and be familiar with the *Governance Handbook*, especially pages 9–13 on the key features of effective governance. It provides the legal framework within which governing bodies must operate.

- If yours is an academy, read and be familiar with the *Academies Financial Handbook* and with your own Articles of Association.
- Consult the chief executive or headteacher, the postholders referred to in the scheme, all staff with existing responsibilities.
- Set out the structure and remit of the board and any committees (including LGBs in a MAT) with the full name of the chair of each.
- Consider what committee structure, if any, is appropriate for your school and create balanced teams by considering the strengths and skills of individuals and matching them to the relevant committees.
- Consider all the powers and responsibilities that will be exercised by the governing board and decide if and to whom they will be delegated and what day-to-day management powers will be delegated to the headteacher.
- Explain the board's parental and community engagement arrangements and how these feed into and inform governance both at board level and at the level of individual schools, as applicable.
- Consider the wording of the preamble to your scheme so that it states clearly when it was approved and how the delegations contained within the framework will operate.
- Adapt an appropriate model scheme of delegation to record your decisions.
- Publish your scheme on your school website (on a webpage without the need to download or open a separate document) in a way that it is easily accessible to all members and governors, clerk, staff, auditors and Ofsted inspectors.
- Review it each September to take account of new governors and/or changes to the committee structure.

Terms of Reference

Terms of reference describe the powers and responsibilities of each committee or LGB. They flow from the decisions you made in drawing up the scheme of delegation and are an essential part of it. It is helpful if all committees and LGBs write their terms of reference to a common, agreed format, although they have to be agreed by the full governing body. Publishing the collected terms of reference to all governors will help to clarify who does what and avoid overlap and misunderstandings.

The following headings provide a good framework for the document: title of committee/LGB; composition and membership; quorum; chairing arrangements; frequency of meetings; minuting and reporting procedures; areas of responsibility; delegated decision-making powers.

A good scheme of delegation is one of those not very exciting documents that you may never fully value or appreciate until something goes wrong and nobody knows where the responsibility and accountability for whatever's gone wrong lies. It's too late to write your scheme after disaster strikes: a scheme of delegation helps to minimise risk.

DAVID MARRIOTT

Making the most of your cash

The government has developed spending advice for schools and is providing some active help with procurement. This includes material specifically for governors.

In the face of a rising chorus of complaints from teacher and headteacher unions and others about the damage to schools caused by shrinking real-term budgets, the government has generally maintained that schools are well funded. Indeed, compared with 25 years ago that is correct, but when it comes to balancing your budget while maintaining a good level of provision, the relevant comparator is not an historic one, but what you got over the last few years. The government's investment in advice services tacitly admits that, despite its protestations, school funding is a problem.

Resource management

Two linked documents, published in May 2018, provide a good starting point for those looking at ways of stretching the budget. *School Resource Management: Checklist* gives eight things to consider:

1. Check how efficient your school is
2. Compare with other schools (financial benchmarking)
3. Checks for financial planning
4. Plan your workforce
5. Get good deals
6. Report to your local authority (for maintained schools)
7. Get financial advice
8. School resource management: training and peer support.

Each point may appear to state the obvious, but helpful practical advice is given for each in links to specific publications. For example, "Plan your workforce" takes you to the DfE's workforce and curriculum planning guidance. The key is in detail: the implicit message is that saving money is not a matter of looking for startling innovation, but doing the obvious, carefully and meticulously.

A document referenced in "Checks for financial planning" contains advice specifically for governors, *School Resource Management: Top 10 planning checks for governors*. Its headings should be considered by any governor committee involved in financial planning or monitoring:

1. Staff pay as percentage of total expenditure
2. Average teacher cost

3. Pupil-to-teacher ratio
4. Class sizes
5. Teacher contact ratio
6. Proportion of budget spent on the leadership team
7. Three- to five-year budget projections
8. Spend per pupil for non-pay expenditure lines compared to similar schools
9. School improvement plan priorities and the relative cost of options
10. List of contracts with costs and renewal dates.

The DfE recommends starting to think about these points early in the planning cycle. Leaving them until you are struggling to finalise a budget where expenditure and income won't meet is too late. They should also underpin planning ahead for three to five years.

Making difficult decisions

The list does not make very comfortable reading as six of the ten points concern staff numbers, and governors usually resist cutting employees, especially teachers. But with staffing costs normally running at up to 80 percent of a school's whole expenditure, looking at this area may well be unavoidable. If you plan ahead you can minimise the effects of staff reductions on the curriculum, and make cuts where they cause least harm, rather being forced by circumstances to quickly do something drastic. Advance planning also enables you to use natural wastage and to avoid making teachers redundant, which is both upsetting for all concerned and often the only achieved after long sessions arguing with teacher unions.

Under each heading *Top 10 Planning Checks* suggests a number of questions for governors to ask. A number of these link to the DfE's benchmarking tools. Looking at what similar schools is doing is always useful. It can prompt analysis of whether you are doing something in the most efficient way, or in a way that has been followed for years without being challenged. But there is also a danger in reacting just to figures. However similar, no two schools are the same, and there may be different factors at work in the schools you are looking at. You should always consider your own school's priorities, look at a range of other schools not only one, and if you can see a real potential saving, ask the senior leadership to contact the schools to find out more about them, what they do and how they cope with their lower spending.

As well as publishing guidance and benchmarking tools, the DfE also runs a procurement help service, Buying for Schools. Your school business manager (SBM) may already be aware of this, but if not they should be encouraged to look at it. It contains training information for financial staff, templates for dealing with suppliers and a memorandum of understanding with Microsoft on discounts on the company's software. Its guidance documents take financial staff step by step through procurement procedures so as to ensure that they are getting good value for money. In addition the Schools Commercial Team recommends a number of deals that are open to schools (www.gov.uk/government/publications/deals-for-schools/deals-for-schools).

Further help from the centre is promised this school year with the launch of a national deal on supply agency fees in late 2018 to reduce agency fees and the finder's fees charged when a school wishes to take on a supply teacher permanently.

Opening horizons

The best help available is working with other schools. Does your business manager have conversations with those in nearby schools like yours? While headteachers are very good at establishing links with other heads, an SBM's job tends to provide fewer opportunities to get out and about. So if they are not having these conversations, ask the headteacher to establish contacts with other SBMs in schools where the two heads have a good relationship. The importance of such working has been championed by Sir David Carter, National Schools Commissioner, who told the Academies Show in April 2018 how important it was for schools to communicate with each other, not only single schools, but also MATs with the aim of working with other MATs. This advice holds good equally for learning from others on the best way of spending what money you get, and in combining on significant purchases. It's a pretty good rule in business that the higher the quantify purchased, the lower the unit price.

You may well feel that your school already knows how to count the pennies and has minimal financial waste. But canny procurement shares much in common with careful planning: both require constant attention and openness to new ideas. You need always to build on what was done last year by realising that things are always a bit different this one.

STEPHEN ADAMSON

Talking points: what efficiency savings?

Isn't it time we ceased to put up with talk about "making efficiency savings" or "squeezing inefficiencies out of the system"? Local authorities have been subject to massive year-on-year cuts for some time, and long since have stopped trimming the fat and instead are cutting into the bone. Schools have been much better protected, but the vast majority are careful with their funds and have known for some years about the advantages of shopping around or making joint purchases with others. Whereas even in the best run organisation there will always be some pounds that could have been better spent, or new ways to be found to get that bit more out of the budget, this is not the same as suggesting there is widespread wastage in the sector. And isn't there a danger of cutting off innovation? Schools progress when teachers discover and get excited by new ideas. To try something new will involve some financial risk, but if you do not experiment you will never make any breakthroughs.

Your equality duties

Many school leaders and governing bodies remain unclear about what the Equality Act 2010 is about and what needs to be done to be compliant.

Search as hard as you like, but you will not find the words "equality policy" in the list of statutory policies and documents that governing boards must have in place. What you will see is the requirement to publish "equality information and objectives". For schools the Equality Act 2010 meant a shift away from ticking boxes and simply having policies to a real commitment to make changes that meet the needs of different groups and tackle disadvantages and inequalities. By having to publish information and identifying what they aim to change or improve, it also means schools are now more accountable.

The current Ofsted *School Inspection Handbook* states that inspectors should consider: "how well leaders and governors promote all forms of equality and foster greater understanding of and respect for people of all faiths (and those of no faith), races, genders, ages, disability and sexual orientations through their words, actions and influence within the school and more widely in the community". One of the core functions of the board is to be the custodian of the school's ethos and values. This means that governors/trustees must ensure that the culture of the school is one that ensures a safe and respectful environment for all learners and staff. There are also implications for the composition of the board and for the school's interaction with parents/carers.

One of the Ofsted grade descriptors for outstanding leadership and management is: "Leaders promote equality of opportunity and diversity exceptionally well, for pupils and staff, so that the ethos and culture of the whole school prevents any form of direct or indirect discriminatory behaviour. Leaders, staff and pupils do not tolerate prejudiced behaviour."

What are schools' legal duties for equality?

The Equality Act requires schools to meet the public sector equality duty. This has two parts: a "general duty" and two "specific duties". The general duty states that a school must have due regard to the need to:

a) eliminate discrimination, harassment, victimisation and any other conduct that is prohibited by the Act

b) advance equality of opportunity between persons who share a relevant protected characteristic and persons who do not share it

c) foster good relations between persons who share a relevant protected characteristic and persons who do not share it.

The protected characteristics are: age, disability, ethnicity and race, gender, gender reassignment, marriage and civil partnership, pregnancy and maternity, religion and belief, and sexual identity and orientation.

The two "specific duties" for schools have been a statutory requirement since 2012. They are:

- To publish equality information at least annually which provides information about the diversity of the school population and how each of the three aspects of the general duty is being met.
- To prepare and publish every four years at least one specific and measurable equality objective which addresses a particular equality issue or challenge.

Key points for governors

Progress towards meeting equality objectives should be regularly monitored through the school development plan (SDP). A more in-depth consideration should be undertaken at least every four years because school contexts can change and schools need to relate to them. Mobility of pupils, staff, governors and families can create a variety of challenges.

It is not just about pupils. It is about all key stakeholders – pupils, staff, governors and parents/carers. In one school in London 80 percent of children were of Indian heritage, split between Brahmins and Dalits (Untouchables). Some Brahmin parents had told their children not to play with the Dalit children. Tackling this would be a long-term challenge for the school, involving changing attitudes and challenging staff, pupils and parents. How could the board play a part in this? Identifying the problem in the SDP, and setting success criteria and milestones at the outset, would prompt action by the school's leadership and provide the framework for monitoring how strategies are implemented and evaluating their impact.

Every person has several protected characteristics. Everyone has an age, an ethnicity, and a religious belief or none. We are male, female, or transgender/transitioning. We may or may not have a disability. We have different sexual orientations. We may be married/in a civil partnership. We may be pregnant or have families. Accordingly, governors need to be well informed about the nature of the diversity within their own school.

Bearing this in mind, questions for governors to ask include:

- What is the profile of the staff – gender, ethnicity, disability, age, etc.? Consider the implications: an article in the *Guardian Teacher Network* bemoaned the fact that when older teachers retire schools lose role models with a wealth of experience. Primary and nursery schools often find it difficult to attract male staff, depriving pupils of a full range of positive role models.
- Is there sufficient flexibility with job share arrangements to support those with young families, and those wanting to approach retirement gradually?
- How fit for purpose is the accessibility plan, and how effective are the reasonable adjustments that must be made for those with a disability?
- What is the gender balance of the senior leadership team?

- Is the pay policy fair?
- What is the profile of pupils – ethnicity, gender, disability, achievement, etc.?
- Are any groups of parents under-represented at school events, including parents' evenings?
- Does the profile of the governing board reflect the community?
- How prepared is the school to support a pregnant student or a child wishing to transition?
- How do we triangulate data to identify which characteristics apply to each child?

Be aware that protected characteristics may overlap with disadvantage. Although disadvantage is itself not a protected characteristic, poverty and deprivation may compound other inequalities. For example, your analysis might identify that boys from a particular ethnic background eligible for free school meals might be underperforming. It might be appropriate then to target Pupil Premium funding to this group.

Fulfilling your specific duties

Publishing information should be handled with sensitivity so that individuals cannot be identified. What goes public may not be totally the same as the information provided for staff and governors.

It is essential that equality objectives are C-SMART. Challenging but specific, measureable, achievable, relevant and time limited. The plan to achieve them should include success criteria and milestones – what do you expect to have achieved by when, in order to hit your end target date? Clarity is needed on who is doing what, the resources required, how and when monitoring of implementation will be undertaken, and how and when the board and external support will evaluate the impact.

Although having one objective is the legal minimum, this is unlikely to be sufficient in most schools. Some examples of objectives are:

- All parts of the building will be accessible to pupils, parents, staff and governors by December 2019.
- The reported incidence of homophobic language will have reduced from "heard often" to "heard rarely" by December 2018.
- The attendance of Somali parents at school events will reflect the proportion of Somali pupils in the school by December 2019.
- The uniform policy will be gender neutral from September 2019.

Final questions

- Has equality information been published and updated in the past year?
- Are the equality objectives published on the school's website?
- Are objectives included in the SDP with success criteria and milestones?
- Does a senior member of staff have responsibility for that element of the plan?
- How are objectives monitored and evaluated by governors?

BILL BOLLOTEN AND MICHELE ROBBINS

Support for disadvantaged pupils

The Pupil Premium does not mean a done deal for tackling the effects of social disadvantage. There is very much more that schools need to do, and the governing board is an important place to look at it.

Removing the attainment gap between pupils from disadvantaged backgrounds and the rest proves to be obstinately difficult, despite the allocation of large amounts of money – the Pupil Premium totals over £2 billion per year, and deprivation is one of the additional needs that feature as a funding block in the new National Funding Formula. Certainly there has been improvement, but the biggest gains, unsurprisingly, were in the first year of the pupil Premium (2011-12), and since then the narrowing of the gap has tailed off. According to DfE statistics, the attainment gap in Key Stage 2 National Curriculum tests in 2017 was 2.99, as opposed to 3.03 the year before. In exams taken at the end of Key Stage 4 it was 3.66 in 2017, a gain of 0.12 on the year before, but this followed two years in which overall the gap actually increased.

Key Stage 4 figures for 2017 look less impressive if you examine Progress 8, which in most people's view is a more important measure than Attainment 8. According to analysis by the FFT Education Datalab the gap between the disadvantaged and the rest widened between 2016 and 2017, notably in English, less so in maths, but with some compensation in a narrowing in other Ebacc subjects.

One should not read too much into the figures for one year, but the pattern shows that gains in bringing the performance of disadvantaged children up to the level of non-disadvantaged ones are hard won. On current rates of progress it will take decades to eliminate the gap entirely. But it is not an immutable law that the differences should always be so large, as other countries do much better. England would have to double the number of disadvantaged pupils achieving top grades in maths to match the best performing nations, and we are firmly in the bottom half of 44 developed nations in this respect. And this is after several years of prioritising the problem.

These are not just cold statistics. They translate into the lives of real young people. *Divergent Pathways*, a report from the Educational Policy Institute, says that at age 16 disadvantaged pupils are educationally 19 months behind their peers, that they are 43 percent less likely to go to university and three times more likely to be on unemployment-related benefits at 19. The gap starts young: it's already two-fifths of the final figure at age five. What is most shocking, though, is that the other three-fifths occur during a child's time at our well-meaning and socially conscious schools.

So what can governors do about it? For if we are committed to producing a more socially equitable society, one of the places to start is the decisions made in the governing board.

Tackling a national problem at school level

The main instrument is clearly the Pupil Premium. Is its diminishing effectiveness because as individual governing boards we are taking it for granted, letting each year's grant be spent the same way as the last, or, worse, just seeing it as a useful contribution to a hard-pressed budget? Do you look at hard at what it is achieving, and challenge how it is being spent? There is plenty of evidence of what works now, especially in the Education Endowment Foundation's *Teaching and Learning Toolkit*, but are you just still employing teaching assistants to support the struggling pupils and regarding that as enough?

Or perhaps the school has fallen into the opposite trap of only using those elements that are high scoring in research or the FFT toolkit? Each school is different, and the measures in the toolkit all work to some degree for some schools. It may well be that you need to try something different and your particular circumstances mean you should test an action even though it is not widely effective elsewhere. The approach should be to start with analysis by your senior leadership of the needs of disadvantaged pupils in your school and then considering a range of possible solutions.

Likewise with looking at other schools. Your school should certainly be casting around for initiatives that work in similar ones. But then how well has it been thought through whether what succeeds down the road will work in your own circumstances?

Do you still look at the annual Pupil Premium statement, or just wave it through? It should contain a considered analysis of what was done last year to support the pupils, not just a list of activities, together with an assessment of its effectiveness. What this says should inform the plan in the report for work in the current year. Has the governing board examined this plan and agreed that it is the right thing to do?

Are you only looking at the Pupil Premium in one committee, with no discussion in the whole governing board? While no one wants to see discussions repeated from committee to full board, the whole board is accountable for the school's educational performance, and everyone should know how the school does in key performance measures, of which the performance of disadvantaged children is one. If this measure shows a lack of improvement, then it is incumbent on each person on the board to be the one to ask why and to challenge what is being done about it.

Complacency is especially likely in a school with only a few disadvantaged pupils. Those schools with the highest numbers of such pupils have done most to close the progress gap, in fact closing it altogether in many primary schools. Where the gap is greatest is in those with the smallest number. But it is no more acceptable to lack concern for these pupils than it would be to turn away from any other minority in the school.

Have a look at the teaching. All research shows that the most effective tool is excellent teaching. Are your best teachers working with disadvantaged children? Have staff considered the barriers to learning among these children, and what can be done about them? One main barrier is the lack of parental involvement in their education, not because they don't care, but because of the simple grinding effects of poverty and the constant struggle to provide the basic support to a family. But that is not a reason not to make contact and to get even tacit support, perhaps by lending books for children to take to a home where there aren't any, or providing a space after school where they can do their homework.

Beyond the Pupil Premium

Initiatives do not stop at spending the Pupil Premium grant. A report from the Education Policy Institute and the Institute of Education found that "countries that achieve both high academic performance and equity between pupils from different backgrounds tend to avoid selection by ability, streaming and setting". Does your school have streaming and setting? As governors, you can abolish these if you think they are impeding the progress of some pupils. You have to be brave.

Consider also your curriculum. For children who come from a home where no one has ever been to college or university, where there are few or no books, where the parents did not enjoy their own schooling, the odds are stacked against academic achievement. But our schools are now encouraged to concentrate on academic subjects, with the primacy given to English and maths and the narrow range of subjects in the Ebacc – which the government wants 90 percent of pupils to take by 2025. However, children who do not excel at the academic subjects may have strong aptitudes in art, music, drama or sport. There are plenty of stories of successful people who struggled at school until they found themselves on a dance floor or a football pitch. They won't get the chance if the school is teaching just the statutory minimum of these subjects, and the message is always being conveyed that these are not the subjects that count. To promote them as fully as needed, your governing board may have to go against the official line and decide that it is not just going to assess success against the formal measures, but that it will prioritise other areas of the curriculum that do not feature or feature so prominently in them. Again, you have to be brave.

Finally, accept that you will never succeed entirely. Many of the problems of social disadvantage are well beyond the control of schools, and often schools are expected to do too much. But schools still have an important part to play, and governors and trustees have a big role in them.

STEPHEN ADAMSON

Addressing mental health and wellbeing

Mental health problems in children are widespread and growing. How well does your school address them?

Half of lifetime mental illnesses start by the age of 14. One in ten children has a clinically diagnosed mental health disorder and/or emotional and behavioural problems (often these are the same children) and one in seven has a mental health/emotional problem that is less severe but which interferes with their development and learning *(Katherine Weare, What Works in Promoting Emotional Wellbeing and Responding to Mental Health Problems in Schools, 2015)*. There is a strong link between student wellbeing, academic attainment and student health. In a recent survey of 7–14 year-olds by GL Assessment 19 percent showed signs of low self-worth and doubted their learning abilities (*Children's Well-being: Pupil attitudes to self and school*). A raft of reports and a government Green Paper (*Transforming Children and Young People's Mental Health Provision*, 2017) show that children's mental health is climbing up the agenda.

Schools already do much to build pupils' resilience, identifying and intervening to address stresses and symptoms before serious mental health problems occur. However, the spotlight on mental health is an opportunity to consider whether more can be done in your school. There are many good practice examples, but while they can be useful they can also lure governors down the line of telling their headteacher what to do. The true role of governing bodies is to establish the school's ethos and hold their headteacher to account through questioning. Governors may expect their senior staff to be aware of the literature, but with so much for heads to do, governors need to focus and ensure that their schools apply the lessons of research.

Professor Katherine Weare's 2015 report highlighted four strands of action for schools to adopt:

1. Adopt whole-school thinking, including: building a supportive school ethos; positive work to promote wellbeing and prevent problems; starting early, identifying difficulties, targeting interventions and sustaining them.
2. Prioritise professional learning and promote staff wellbeing.
3. Engage the whole community – consult pupils and parents.
4. Develop supportive policy on tackling prejudice and stigma around mental health.

Adopt whole-school thinking and develop a supportive policy

If your ethos statement recognises the importance of laying the foundations for good mental health, you can ask for reports on how the curriculum promotes resilience and develops pupils' understanding of mental health, including removing the stigma of mental illness. The PSHE Association publishes guidance and lesson plans for schools on preparing to teach about mental health and emotional wellbeing (*Guidance on Preparing to Teach about Mental Health and Emotional Well-being*, 2016); these start early, with Key Stage 1, and work through all age groups.

Schools will be aware of the many factors which contribute to student anxiety at different ages and stages. Some of these are intrinsic to school: challenging learning, tests and exams, peer pressure, and bullying. The state of the toilets can also be an issue: the charity Sanitation First reports that 73 percent of UK children are unhappy with the state of their school toilets, and a shocking 20 percent have admitted that this problem had prompted them to stay at home (*School Toilets: Why Settle For Bog Standard?*, 2018). There is a link between anxiety and physical health: in an attempt to avoid school toilets, some children don't drink enough water during the day, which increases their risk of dehydration and bladder infections. These problems affect learning as well. It is an anxiety that schools could remove by better cleaning, maintenance and supervision – something that governors can easily check on.

Others problems stem from family circumstances, whether long term, like poverty, or unexpected events such as bereavement, or from life changes and transitions; yet others from externals such as the news, advertising and internet. School policy and practice can mitigate or help pupils to navigate those challenges. Children's self-esteem may be damaged by embarrassment over the clothes and equipment they bring to school when compared with their better-off peers. Non-uniform days may be a fun way of raising funds for charities but if some pupils flaunt designer labels it can throw economic disparities into high relief.

Despite the school's best efforts there will be some students who suffer mental illness. If the school has been successful in removing the stigma of mental illness, pupils and parents will be more ready to inform the school and other pupils will be more understanding when problems arise. The Green Paper suggested that every school should have a Designated Senior Lead for Mental Health to oversee the approach to mental health and wellbeing. While early identification of difficulties would be part of routine pastoral work, the Designated Senior Lead, like a SENCO, would take responsibility for pupils when referrals to outside agencies including Child and Adolescent Mental Health Services become appropriate.

Prioritise professional learning

While school staff are not expected to become experts, without an understanding of mental health issues they will not be equipped to identify and start to address pupils' needs. A whole staff approach may avoid thoughtless remarks which reinforce the stigma of mental illness. The Green Paper suggests that every school should aim to have at least one member of staff trained in mental health first aid.

Engage the whole community

Governors can be involved in consulting the student voice about what works well and what could be improved to promote pupil well-being. Participating in discussions with students conveys its seriousness, aids governor understanding and may identify a factor that the school has overlooked. Governors can explain through school newsletters their ethos statement if it prioritises mental health. Schools that value parents as co-educators of their children will provide opportunities to listen to parents' concerns and help to develop consistent messages and actions about, for example motivating children to do their best, encouraging healthy sleep patterns, restricting screen time and trying to prevent access to harmful internet images.

In one school, governors initiated a forum for parents of Year 10 pupils to meet informally and discuss issues like getting their children to organise their homework and revision timetabling. A senior teacher was in attendance to give advice when called upon. Then discussion naturally broadened out to dealing with a broader range of issues about adolescence. This could have happened just as well if the meeting had been led by the head.

Questions governors might ask

- Would it be helpful for school leaders to work through the National Children's Bureau's eight-page self-assessment and improvement tool for school leaders, *A Whole School Framework for Emotional Well-Being and Mental Health* (2016)?
- How does the school teach about resilience and mental health?
- What have we learned from consulting pupils?
- How successful are the school's efforts to enlist the support of parents?
- What aspects of pupils' anxiety has the school identified for improvement?
- How well does the school ameliorate pressures caused by long-term family circumstances or unexpected challenges?
- Are there sufficient resources, including staff time and training, for the identification of problems and to provide appropriate interventions?
- Where referral to outside professionals or CAMHS is appropriate, is the response time acceptable? Would it be helpful for the governing body to lobby on this?

MARTIN POUNCE

New training for chairs

New DfE endorsed training has been designed to deliver the same goals whoever provides it, but there is a wide choice of styles on offer.

In January 2018 the DfE announced that it had issued contracts to five organisations to deliver and develop new training for chairs of governing bodies and trusts.

The training replaces the Chairs of Governing Bodies Development Programme, which had been in place since 2012. It was due for an overhaul because of the changes that have taken place in governance since then. It is not just in content that the new programme differs from the old one, developed by the National College of Teaching and Leadership: the National College training was a single programme delivered under licence by various providers around the country. The providers could tweak it if they wished and add their own regional differences, but it was essentially the same course wherever you took it. However, the new providers have developed their own courses and their own methods of delivery, so where you take the course will be significant. There are also variations in cost.

This does not mean, however, that you will be offered chalk in one place and cheese in another. All the courses had to be based closely on the Competency Framework for Governance (https://assets.publishing.service.gov.uk/government/uploads/system/uploads/attachment_data/file/583733/Competency_framework_for_governance_.pdf). The contracts have therefore been awarded to those providers who found the best ways of guiding chairs to acquire the six features of effective governance from which the competencies derive, with a view also to allowing variety and choice.

Providers

Three of the five providers deliver the course nationally, while the other two cover a large part of the country between them. You can therefore choose between three or four, depending on where you live. The five providers have very different characteristics:

- GovernorSpace – set up by Entrust Support Services, based in Stafford; www.governorspace.co.uk; delivered nationally
- FASNA, in partnership with Ambition School Leadership – FASNA is a national network of schools, predominantly academies and foundation schools; www.fasna.org.uk/conferences/governance-programmes/the-governance-leadership-programme; delivered nationally
- The National Governance Association (NGA) – www.nga.org.uk; delivered nationally

- Govern Ed – a private limited company based in London that supplies educational support services; www.govern-ed.co.uk; delivered in the South East, East and London
- The Alliance of Leading Learning – a school-led partnership based in Shropshire; www.leadinglearning.co.uk/free-governance-training; delivered in Lancashire, West Yorkshire and the West Midlands.

Three providers – the NGA, the Alliance of Leading Learning, and FASNA – deliver a mix of face-to-face and online training, spreading the course out over a number of months and letting participants develop at their own pace. Govern Ed's course is three face-to-face workshops, each lasting three hours and spread across three half-terms, with no online element. In contrast, GovernorSpace works entirely through distance learning.

Govern Ed also differs from the other providers by running two separate courses, one for members of MAT trusts and the other for governors of maintained schools, single academy trusts or local governing committees. Up to four trustees can attend the MAT training, one of whom should be the chair or vice-chair, and two governors the single-school course, one of whom should already have a chairing role on the board or be aspiring to move to one.

FASNA restricts attendance to chairs of maintained schools, but allows academies to send any trustee. Other providers make it clear that the course is intended for existing or aspiring chairs. For example, the NGA's course is called Development for Chairs.

In all courses, the participants' needs are assessed at the start of the process, whether by self-evaluation or a 360° evaluation. All courses also incorporate production of an action plan for the governing board, giving the participant a practical outcome to take back in order to develop the whole board. This indicates a strong degree of personalisation, aided between workshops by the support of a mentor.

The balance between face-to-face training and online training is similar amongst the three providers that follow this route. Basically, the face-to-face element addresses the six key features of effective leadership in the Competency Framework, whether paired across three workshops (NGA), as either six twilight sessions or three full-day ones (Alliance of Leading Learning) or as part of eight core topics in an intensive two-day residential (FASNA).

Online training is more tailored to the participant's own development needs. The Alliance of Leading Learning offers six optional topics, and the NGA access to its range of e-learning modules. FASNA's five online modules are a non-discretionary part of the course, but it also offers optional additional masterclasses.

GovernorSpace (which is all online) operates a different model. Boards receive a number of credits, which are used to access interactive online training (webinars), bespoke training for the governing body or mentor support, according to the wishes of the participant. Governing boards of

MATs, federations or schools in Opportunity Areas that have been judged to require improvement or be coasting receive more credits than other schools.

Overall, with the workshops, online training and development of an action plan, participants can expect the work to last over 6 months (Govern Ed) or nine months to a year (the others).

Financial support

The DfE is supporting the cost of the training through grants of £500. In the case of the NGA, the Alliance of Leading Learning and Govern Ed this covers the entire cost. Other governors from the board can also participate in the Alliance's training at a payment of £450. The grant provides six credits for maintained schools and standalone academies on the GovernorSpace training, but governing boards of MATs or federations or those of schools in Opportunity Areas that have been judged to require improvement or coasting get 18. One credit buys a place on a webinar, three a mentoring session, and six bespoke training for the whole governing board.

FASNA's course, reflecting the residential element, is more costly, totalling £1700 of which £500 is covered by the grant. However, it is free for MAT boards governing two or more schools, or single schools located in an Opportunity Area and rated "requires improvement" or identified as "coasting"; these boards also receive a voucher worth £300 to purchase bespoke elements of support for a chair or the Board.

Those thinking of participating should be able to find a course that matches their own prefered learning style. Not everybody takes well to on-line learning, whereas for some people it is ideal, enabling them to fit training into a hectic life at their own time. Whichever course is followed is, though, going to involve a serious time commitment, which is how it should be given the nature of the role you are undertaking. When considering the course you also, obviously, need to consider geography and whether the face-to-face courses are being held near you. But it is also important to look at the provider's website and reflect on whether their provision is best intended for your type of school and think about the nature of the likely other participants. At any face-to-face learning you should expect to be able to learn from your fellow attenders and establish some supportive contacts.

HARRIET MANSON

────── Talking points: redirect training support ──────

Government money spent on governor training is always welcome, but the current emphasis only looks at one end of the scale. You can get grants to cover the cost of chairs' training, but the government will not make induction training compulsory for new governors. Isn't that where the money is most needed, to help new governors hit the ground running?

New training for clerks

Like the new training course for chairs (see previous pages), the DfE-approved training for clerks, which started in spring 2018, is available from a number of providers, who provide a variety of styles and locations.

Five contracts were awarded to develop and deliver new training for clerks:

- FASNA, in partnership with Ambition School Leadership – www.fasna.org.uk/conferences/governance-programmes/the-governance-leadership-programme; delivered nationally
- The National Governance Association (NGA) – www.nga.org.uk; delivered nationally
- GovernorSpace – set up by Entrust Support Services in Stafford; www.governorspace.co.uk; delivered nationally
- Hampshire County Council – www.hants.gov.uk/professionalclerk; delivered in the South West and the South East, incorporating south London
- School Development Support Agency (SDSA) – www.letslearn.org.uk/cpd-and-training; delivered in all regions apart from the South West, the South East and south London.

The organisations represent a spectrum of those engaged in clerking and governance. Hampshire County Council has a track record in developing clerks training and for some years have been running a clerks' accreditation programme. GovernorSpace also has roots in local authority provision, having been set up by Entrust Support Services with a commission from Staffordshire County Council to provide school improvement services, and works with a number of other local authorities.

FASNA and the NGA are third sector organisations. FASNA is a national network of schools, predominantly academies and foundation schools, while the NGA will be familiar to all clerks and governors. The SDSA is a not-for-profit organisation whose major area of expertise is the organisation of training and development for those working in schools and in children's services.

A range of programmes

Unlike the previous national training for clerks, there is no single programme that the trainers are all expected to deliver. Instead, the DfE invited organisations to tender for developing a course that was based on the four key features of professional clerking that form the basis of the Clerking Competency Framework. It was up to the bidders to develop their own way of best fulfilling this aim. To be successful they had to develop a course that was "about professionalising the quality of clerking support available to governing boards". Two outcomes were sought:

increasing clerking expertise and involving clerks in peer-to-peer support networks. While the offers differ in significant ways, the brief does ensure a lot of common ground and, most importantly, common aims.

All providers apart from GovernorSpace build their courses around face-to-face sessions, dubbed modules or workshops, which address the four key features. The NGA and SDSA do this in four half-day sessions, followed in the NGA's case by a school-based project. FASNA provides two half-day workshops and eight on-line modules. Hants also offers two-half day workshops followed by online modules, but participants can instead do the whole course in six online modules if they prefer.

All courses start with a self-evaluation or 360° evaluation, which is used to steer the participant to choose the options they need. After the evaluation a clerk on the GovernorSpace course is guided by a mentor in the choice of which five hour-long webinars they will take from those available. All of these are related to the 16 competencies in the Framework. Where relevant there are alternative modules for academies and maintained schools.

All courses include mentor or facilitator support, whether at the beginning to help the participant with choices, or throughout the course.

Finding the right course for you

A grant from the DfE of £350 is available for all participants. The programme is delivered at no additional cost by GovernorSpace, while Hampshire charge schools an additional £50, the NGA and FASNA £75 and the SDSA £80.

The time involved is one term with the SDSA, one to two terms with Hampshire, about two terms with the NGA, two to three terms with GovernorSpace. FASNA's course, which has been developed in association with the Institute of School Business Leadership and Chartered Institute for Public Finance and Accountancy, is expected to take about a year.

All providers state that the clerks participating should be experienced, but this could mean only a few months. Before signing up, interested clerks should also look at the websites to see where the face-to-face sessions are being delivered. Some providers offer a good geographical spread, but in some of the others the choice of locations is very limited. It is also worth looking at the add-ons: for example, the NGA gives you access to a number of additional e-learning modules, FASNA provides a learning log for you to fill in, on completing Hampshire's course you can move on to the Accredited Clerk's programme, SDSA's builds in inter-session research, and GovernorSpace gives you access to a peer-to-peer support database. Before committing, clerks should also decide on the breadth of the training they feel they need. Do I need a good grounding in a wide area of clerking expertise, or just in some areas? If the former, you don't want to find that some options are not open to you, and if the latter that you are spending time on things you know a lot about already.

STEPHEN ADAMSON

Clerking – It's all in the planning and preparation...

The NGA Outstanding Clerk of 2017 gives her views on what a clerk can do to help raise the standards of a governing board and help governors to think ambitiously.

Working for a number of schools over the course of several years I have been fortunate to pick up good practice to share with my governing boards. This means we can develop and work within a framework of continual self-improvement and self-reflection.

Planning and evaluation

With some of my schools I meet on a termly basis with the headteacher and chair of governors and sometimes with the committee chairs to plan the term's work. I plan and organise the work of the governing board using a meeting planner. I have also developed a rolling policy review schedule so that we know which policies are assigned to which committees and when they are due for review.

I have developed analytical skills by conducting 360-degree chair's reviews, analysing the results and sharing the sometimes sensitive feedback, firstly, with my chairs of governors and then with the governing board (after the chair has checked that they are happy for further circulation). Often learning and development points emerge from them for the chairs and the governors in terms of increasing understanding about what the role involves.

When it comes to governor self-evaluation I assist by facilitating governor training sessions, focusing on the *Twenty Questions Every Governing Board Should Ask Itself* (see pages 78–9), and from the outcome develop a governing board action plan to focus on areas for improvement. This is good for team-building and promoting shared responsibility for the growth of the governing board.

Attending a course on mediation a few years ago helped me to develop mediation skills. Often I find myself a sounding board for the headteacher, chair of governors and other members of the governing board, particularly around governor relationships and other sensitive issues.

Between meetings

Support and challenge to the SLT are, of course, central to what governors do, so I aim to help them by identifying, encouraging and booking them on pertinent training where they can learn what questions they should be asking. This is reinforced by self-reflection at each governing board meeting. We always end by asking ourselves, "What have we done in our meeting to impact on the children of our school?"

Between meetings governor accountability and improved communication are reinforced by using feedback documents such as a training cascade form so that governors can evaluate the courses that they have been on and report back on what they have learned and what needs to be implemented as a result. We also have focused link governor feedback report forms for them to complete once they have undertaken a visit, documenting the focus and impact of the visit.

During meetings

At the start of meetings, we elect by rotation one governor as a timekeeper and one as a meeting reviewer; the latter uses a tick list and comment box throughout the duration of the meeting to grade different aspects of it, such as the quality and timeliness of supporting papers and presentation, management of the meeting, whether there has been wide participation from attendees and whether actions are clear. Feedback is given at the end of the meeting.

I also encourage headteachers to send their termly report out early and for governors to read and submit questions in advance so that the headteacher can answer them ahead of the meeting. These are then attached as Q&As to the minutes and provide evidence of support and challenge. Governors take it in turns to collate an executive summary of committee minutes and link governor reports which is distributed in advance of a GB meeting (full committee minutes are available to all governors). This also helps us to streamline the agendas and work "smart".

Going further

There are many more things you can do to help your governing board, though these will not be open to all clerks. Over the years I have delivered briefings and training courses for new clerks and for governors about valuing and getting the most of their clerks. Having also clerked a number of hearings over time I have co-facilitated training sessions for governors and clerks on how to conduct a hearing.

It also helps if you have experience of working with schools in capacities other than clerking, providing these develop your understanding of the education processes while not conflicting with the role as clerk. For one of my schools, I have the insight of minuting admin team meetings, staff meetings, pupil focus meetings and post-16 leavers questionnaire meetings. For the partnership of schools that I work for I co-ordinate and minute the half-termly curriculum group meetings that cover the broad curriculum areas of SEND/Inclusion, ICT and Computing, English, Maths, RE, PE, EYFS and Science. I am also helping the groups to develop an impact report for the headteachers in the partnership so that they can demonstrate the importance of the schools meeting and sharing good practice.

ANGIE MARCHANT

Making codes of conduct work effectively

Expectations of codes of conduct, and their effectiveness in improving governing body practice, have moved on considerably in recent years.

The last time this Yearbook looked at codes of conduct was in 2010 when the idea of formalising a code setting out the expectations, behaviours and commitment necessary for good governance was much more tentative than it is now. Models then focused on using codes as a helpful tool to address some of the common frustrations of managing inappropriate governor behaviour, such as governors who were unable to work as part of a team, who worked against the ethos of the school or who failed to commit and contribute to the work of the governing body. Codes of conduct that set out expectations were seen as a useful tool for the chair to use as a basis for having difficult conversations with such problematic individuals.

In the last eight years things have developed a great deal. There is now a clear expectation from the Department for Education (DfE) that governing boards will agree a formal code of conduct, and the recently updated draft code from the National Governance Association (NGA) is referred to in DfE documentation. Although codes are not a legal requirement, the statutory guidance supporting the School Governance Constitution Regulations 2012 states, "A code of conduct should be maintained and communicated to all prospective governors to set clear expectations of the governors' role and behaviour." This guidance is for maintained schools and, as it is statutory, governing boards must follow it unless they have good reason not to. There is an expectation that academies should follow suit as the *Governance Handbook*, which applies to both academies and maintained schools, confirms that governing boards and trust boards should have a code of conduct.

The *Governance Handbook* talks of codes setting out clear expectations of professional behaviour and giving an outline of effective governance that is shared with new governors during recruitment and induction. It states that "explicit agreement to the code of conduct will mean there is a common reference point should any difficulties arise in the future". The handbook emphasises the use of the code to make it clear that governors should attend training. It also states that, where a governor or trustee fails to meet training expectations, a code of conduct can be used to suspend them on the basis of bringing the role into disrepute.

Getting the code right

So is the focus of codes to address poor behaviour or can they be used in a more positive way to promote effective governance? Clearly setting out high expectations and standards of professional behaviour that have been agreed by the board can have a positive impact on future governor/trustee behaviour. All governors, established and new to the board, are reminded of their commitment and responsibilities.

What is included in a code is discretionary so, once the basics are covered, there is scope to add particular areas relevant to an individual board: for example, an agreed section on the school ethos for schools of a religious character or agreed expectations for behaviour at meetings where these have not always been professional.

The comprehensive 2017 NGA model code (www.nga.org.uk/ codeofconduct2017) outlines the purpose of the board and describes the relationships between individuals, the whole board and the leadership team of the school. This new model updates and extends the 2015 versions that many governing boards are still using. It combines the old maintained school and academy models into one example that both governing boards and trust boards can use as a sound basis from which to work. The language has been updated to take into account new school and leadership structures, and it encourages boards to customise as appropriate. For example, it recognizes that some trustees will be involving themselves in governance of more that one school. Key additions have been made to the roles and responsibilities section where the role of governor/trustee in relation to senior leaders is set out explicitly and where the responsibility of governors/trustees to reflect the views of the board and not undermine collective decision-making is clearly stated. There is also a stronger emphasis on the need for confidentiality and courtesy, and for the first time the latter is specifically extended to dealings with clerks.

Summary

Building a positive, professional and productive working environment takes effort, and a clear, well-used code of conduct for governors/trustees can play a significant part in establishing it. This should involve reviewing the code annually as part of the more general review of the board's effectiveness. The board can only work better if all members plus school leaders and the clerk understand the content and if board members sign the code as a formal recognition that they have read it and will abide by its content.

DAVID MARRIOTT

Talking points: board diversity

The NGA has rightly launched a campaign to increase the diversity on governing boards. Conversely, the DfE wants to see "skilled" people from business and the professions on boards. In practice this often means middle managers and above. Socially this means little diversity, and given the current biases in our society, ethnically it means little diversity too. It appears that the one aim works against the other.

Providing effective challenge

Providing good challenge is still the heart of governance, at whatever level, but without guidance it remains hard to get right.

School governors are expected to hold professional school leaders to account for standards and progress in their schools by challenging them on the basis of data and other evidence. To any fair-minded observer this must seem a difficult, if not impossible task. It is not a contest of equals. The head who wants to minimise or deflect challenge has many options to do so, while the governor who seeks to challenge robustly faces formidable obstacles.

Nevertheless, "challenge" is the right word, especially when balanced with the word "support". Much depends on the motivation and intention that lies behind the challenge. If governors are there to protect and promote the best interests of the children and young people, even over the interests of the staff, then this will mean challenging staff assumptions, behaviour and attitudes from time to time. At the same time, it must be recognised that good headteachers challenge themselves continually and welcome challenge from other people, including governors.

The human dimension is rarely considered by the DfE in their advice and guidance to governors. In fact, in every school the relationship between the governors and the leadership team must be carefully grown over time. The boundaries of their respective roles need to be understood and respected, and mutual expectations must be realistic. But all the advice, training and guidance in the world won't make the slightest difference if the relationship between the governors and the school leadership team is dysfunctional. If challenge is to be regular and effective, that relationship has to be disinterestedly professional, each group respecting the other.

Strategies for effective challenge

• **Get it right** – ask the right question at the right time in the right forum of the right person in the right way.

Effective challenge can depend on a lot of different and sometimes conflicting factors. The right question at the wrong time or in the wrong forum can lead to an unsatisfactory outcome. The right question asked in the wrong tone of voice can be counterproductive. The right question asked of the wrong person won't lead to the answer you need.

• **Don't underestimate yourselves.** The quality of governance and the skills, experience and behaviours of governors have been improving steadily in recent years, in part due to the DfE's insistence on the appropriate skills being the main qualification for being a governor rather than representation. Many governors now bring to the role high-level, sophisticated skills and abilities that can be applied very effectively in the school and governance context. Objectivity is vital.

• **Be clear about your motivation.** Make sure there's no personal agenda. If you dislike or disapprove of the head, and especially if this is known, it's probably best if someone else pursues the challenge so that it cannot be misinterpreted as a personal attack or vendetta.

• **Base it on objective evidence and use objective evidence to pursue it.** What facts have you got at your disposal? Are you fully confident of the grounds of your challenge? If you anticipate a glib or superficial answer, have you prepared follow-up questions based on the same or further evidence?

• **Don't give up after one question: be persistent but don't nag.** It is often the third or fourth question that really gets at the truth. Professionals are good at answering initial and immediate follow-up questions. Be prepared to ask a series of questions, but this must be balanced with awareness of the effect of persistent questioning on the head and others involved.

• **Seek allies and prepare.** It is easier to pursue a challenge if you are confident that others are with you. It is dangerous to assume this rather than talking to colleagues in advance to find out where they stand on a particular issue. Preparation is vital. Do your research. Check the facts. Think about the timing of your questions. Phrase your questions with care. Make sure you have evidence to hand, in case you are challenged yourself. Identify your allies.

• **Be firm and clear but not aggressive.** Asking a well-crafted question is a sophisticated skill. Forensic questioning is well-targeted, carefully phrased and allows very little room for evasion. Politeness and respect are an important element of this. The more aggressive the questioning, the less likely it is that you will get to the truth. Don't confuse aggression with persistence and assertiveness. Be prepared to recognise the truth when you see it, even if it conflicts with any presuppositions. Be big enough to admit that you are wrong, when it's appropriate.

• **Know your rights.** Challenging (balanced with support) is absolutely central to the governor's role. It is more than legitimate – it is vital. Heads should expect it and see it as healthy, and a part of the process of improving the school.

• **Consider why you may not be getting the answers you need.** When put under pressure, most people are liable to behave defensively or seek to avoid the situation through a variety of deflecting actions. This is especially so if their weaknesses are exposed, or are in danger of being exposed. When people are tired or have had a particularly challenging day they are less likely to respond well to even well-meant and gentle questioning. Ask yourself whether you can see a developing pattern of behaviour. Understanding human behaviour is a lifelong task but most of us are reasonably skilled at seeing what lies beneath the surface. So it's important to be sensitive to the head's frame of mind and to empathise with them – but this should not deter us from ever asking a tough question.

• **Don't store up unsatisfied challenges.** If governors do not get satisfactory answers to their questions over a significant period of time, there can be a dangerous build-up of frustration which can suddenly explode. This may be cathartic but might also be very damaging to individuals and the effective maintenance of a good working relationship between head and governors. Nipping this in the bud is the best way forward. A good chair will sense a developing problem and seek advice and peer support in addressing it before it becomes a crisis.

• **Appoint a professional clerk.** As the *Clerking Competency Framework* (DfE, April 2017) says: "Professional clerking plays a crucial role in supporting the board to hold executive leaders to account... Professional clerking also informs the board's accountability to others through minutes that provide evidence of challenge and scrutiny of the executive, and the board's overall ability and capacity to govern the organisation well."

• **Seek external validation and advice.** Getting a second opinion from an expert can be very helpful but isn't always easy to achieve and may cost the school money. Nonetheless, this is less expensive than having the school go into Special Measures because the governors didn't notice what was going wrong.

• **Access training.** It is important for at least some of the governing board to undertake relevant training in giving support and challenge in order to boost the board's collective confidence in raising legitimate questions. Other forms of training that increase the board's knowledge, and hence make challenge better informed, are also necessary.

• **Talk to other governors from other schools.** One important side benefit of attending governor training is meeting governors from different schools and sharing problems and solutions. But this can be achieved in a variety of other ways, too, such as online and via social media. Schools are remarkably different from each other and develop different cultures and practices over time. Finding out that other governors experience the same issues as you can be reassuring. Finding out that what your school does is very different from most others can be good, if the outcomes are brilliant, or worrying if not. Either way, you go away feeling wiser.

DAVID MARRIOTT

David's book Challenge: How governors can challenge school leaders effectively *is available from Adamson Publishing (www.adamsonbooks. com)*

Briefings

Government to look at improving governance

In May 2018 the DfE published a policy paper stating the principles of how they would hold schools to account, *Principles for a Clear and Simple Accountability System*. As well as discussing the roles of Ofsted and Regional School Commissioners (RSCs) (see below), this paper also stated that the department will "focus on how we can improve the effectiveness of governance in the sector more generally, including at MAT level". MATs are singled out for particular attention because they are growing in number and are still evolving.

Coasting schools and floor standards measures to merge

At a speech given to the NAHT in May 2018, the Secretary of State for Education, Damian Hinds, said that it was confusing to have two separate measures holding schools to account for their performance, and that the floor standards and the judgement of coasting would be combined into a single measure. He set no date for this to happen, but said a consultation on how to replace them would be launched in the autumn.

He also said that only an Ofsted judgement of inadequate would trigger the forced academisation of maintained schools.

The government is going to clarify the inspection of schools, and that this responsibility would rest solely with Ofsted. Currently in some circumstances RSCs can send advisers into schools to assess their performance.

DBS disclosures for MAT chairs

It is now mandatory for all academy chairs of trusts to have their application for a DBS enhanced disclosure certificate countersigned by the Secretary of State for Education. All new chairs are required to have a new enhanced DBS certificate, regardless of positions held previously at a different trust. There is an exemption for chairs of trusts who already have an enhanced DBS certificate from a school that is converting to an academy trust.

The procedure is given in www.gov.uk/guidance/enhanced-dbs-disclosure-checks-for-chairs-of-academy-trusts.

Revised statutory safeguarding guidance

A new edition of *Keeping Children Safe in Education* became applicable at the beginning of this school year. This guidance, which schools must follow, has been designed to be clearer than its predecessor, and contains new advice on handling allegations of child-on-child sexual violence and sexual harassment.

New technical qualification

The precedence of academic subjects over technical ones has long been criticised in our schools, and now the government is aiming to redress the balance by introducing new qualifications in technical subjects: T Levels. These are two-year, technical programmes for 16–18 year-olds designed in partnership with employers. Learning will be through a mixture of classroom or workshop-based teaching and on-the-job experience in various industries, including a placement of at least 45 days in the student's chosen industry or occupation. They will be taught from 2020.

Reception baseline assessment to start

The design and delivery of a new system of assessing children at the start of primary school has been commissioned by the DfE from the National Foundation for Educational Research (NFER). A 20-minute teacher assessment will look at language, literacy and early mathematical skills. The results will not be passed on to individual parents, but will be aggregated and used to judge how well primary schools help children progress across their time with them.

The system will be trialled this school year, piloted in 2019–20, and be fully instituted in schools in autumn 2020.

The last attempt to introduce baseline acceptance collapsed in 2016 when the three companies contracted by the DfE delivered incompatible systems.

Health education to become compulsory

The DfE announced in July that it was planning to make health education compulsory in September 2020. At the same time it published draft guidance on how it and relationships education should be taught.

What parents tell Ofsted

The Ofsted Parents Panel annual report for 2017, published in spring 2018, summarised the views passed on by parents. These include:

- Parents widely complained that there is an excessive focus on English and maths in the key stage 2 curriculum and SATs, with the result that humanities and art often miss out.
- Most parents of secondary school age children (87 percent) consider homework helpful to their children. The approval rate for primary school homework is smaller, at 64 percent.
- A lot of parents complained that Early Years reports read as if not written for them but for professionals, with the language over-technical and heavy with jargon.

Ofsted undertook to consider parents' views when developing inspection, but is not committed to acting on them.

Academy pay and contracts to be subject to greater scrutiny

Damian Hinds, Secretary of State for Education, used his first major speech on governance to announce that there would be more transparency in the pay of top earners in academies. He told the NGA summer conference in June 2018 that academy accounts would have to publish details of staff earning over £100,000 and the percentage of teaching time undertaken by these individuals.

New financial requirements on academies

As well as introducing an expectation that academy trust boards meet more than three times a year (see page 69), the 2018 edition of the *Academies Financial Handbook* tightens up trust accounting procedures. Trusts must now not just produce management accounts but give them to their chairs each month. These must be examined at each board meeting. The board should particularly look at any variations between budgeted income and expenditure.

The Handbook enforces the transparent and proportionate approach to senior executive pay promised in the Secretary of State's speech to the NGA, requiring trusts to be able to justify how they make their decisions. The ESFA may challenge pay levels it deems inappropriate. Trusts must also publish their gender pay gap.

This move to clamp down on excessive pay awards is coupled with a requirement from April 2019 that all related party transactions (contracts with companies in whom a trust member, their family or business has an interest) be declared to the Education and Skills Funding Agency and that trusts seek approval for any such transactions over £20,000.

More DfE money for governor training

In his June 2018 speech to the NGA Damian Hinds promised to double the DfE's budget for governor and trustee training to £6 million up to 2021.

Free job advertising

Promised over two years ago, a free website for advertising job vacancies in schools has been piloted by the DfE and was pledged for national roll out in autumn 2018.

Diversity on the board

The DfE is committed to trying to increase representation of ethnic minorities in senior position in schools through its Equality and Diversity Fund. The NGA recognises that there is a similar problem on governing boards, with only 4 percent of governors who take part in its governance survey identifying themselves as from ethnic minorities. Believing that it is important for governing boards to reflect their communities, the NGA has launched the Everyone on Board Campaign, in the hope that boards will do more to encourage volunteers from ethnic minorities.

part two

Planning and Resources

2019

Information sources

Key government publications

The Governance Handbook, DfE

The Academies Financial Handbook, DfE

The School Governance (Roles, Procedures and Allowances) (England) Regulations 2013: departmental advice for school leaders and governing boards of maintained schools and management committees of PRUs in England, DfE

Common Inspection Framework: education, skills and early years, Ofsted

School Inspection Handbook, Ofsted

School Inspection Handbook – section 8, Ofsted

Timelines for schools, both "mandatory" and "useful", DfE

All on www.gov.uk.

Also http://researchbriefings.parliament.uk includes a series of unbiased summaries of educational topics.

Academies

General information is available from the Department for Education, www.gov.uk, including FAQs for those considering conversion

Advice for governors on converting to an academy is also available for NGA members on its website, www.nga.org.uk.

The Charity Commission, www.gov.uk/government/organisations/charity-commission, has details of academies' obligations as charities and advice on trusteeship. Academies should file their annual returns on this site

DfE, *Multi-Academy Trusts: Good practice guidance and expectations for growth* sets out design principles for academy trusts, including new trusts and existing trusts planning to grow. It also provides examples of good practice, www.gov.uk/government/uploads/system/uploads/attachment_data/file/576240/Multi-academy_trusts_good_practice_guidance_and_expectations_for_growth.pdf

FASNA (Freedom and Autonomy for Schools – National Association) is a national network for academies and MATs, www.fasna.org.uk

NCTL, *Governance in Multi-Academy Trusts*, www.gov.uk/government/publications/governance-in-multi-academy-trusts

NGA, *Model Schemes of Delegation*, www.nga.org.uk/Guidance/School-structures-and-constitution/Academies-and-free-schools/New-Model-Schemes-of-Delegation.aspx

RSA Academies Commission, *Unleashing Greatness: Getting the best from an academised system*, www.thersa.org>Action and research>Learning, cognition and creativity>Education

Admissions

DfE, *School Admissions Code*, www.gov.uk

Appointing and recruiting staff

DfE & NGA, *Recruiting a Headteacher*, www.gov.uk/government/publications/recruiting-a-headteacher

NGA, *Headteacher Recruitment Toolkit*, www.nga.org.uk/Guidance/Finance-and-Staffing/Executive-and-Senior-leadership/Headteacher-Recruitment-Toolkit.aspx

See also SAFEGUARDING

Appraisal

DfE, *Teacher Appraisal and Capability – A model policy for schools*, also gives guidance

NGA & NCOGS, *Knowing your School: Governors and staff performance*, www.nga.org.uk/Resources/Knowing-Your-School.aspx

David Spicer *et al.*, *Effectively Managing Headteacher Performance*, NCTL, 2014, www.gov.uk

Arts

Artsmark, Arts Council England's programme for schools to evaluate and strengthen their arts and cultural provision, www.artsmark.org.uk

Arts Award, arts award for individual young people, www.artsaward.org.uk

Bullying

DfE, *Bullying at School*, www.gov.uk/bullying-at-school

Ofsted, *No Place for Bullying*, www.gov.uk/government/publications/school-strategies-for-preventing-and-tackling-bullying

Careers advice

DfE, *Careers Guidance and Access for Education and Training Providers*, statutory guidance, www.gov.uk/government/publications/careers-guidance-provision-for-young-people-in-schools

Chairing

NGA, *Chair's Handbook, The*, revised edition 2017

NGA and National College, *Leading Governors: The role of the chair of governors in schools and academies*, www.gov.uk/government/publications/leading-governors-the-role-of-the-chair-of-governors

There are five providers of the Governance Leadership Development programme. A list is on www.gov.uk/government/publications/licensees-professional-development-for-school-governors

Charging and school visits

DfE, *Charging for School Activities*, departmental advice

Child protection

Various documents are published by the DfE on www.gov.uk, including *Keeping Children Safe in Education*

See also SAFEGUARDING

Clerks

Clerkwise, regularly updated on-line information service for clerks, www.adamsonbooks.com

DfE, *Clerking Competency Framework*, www.gov.uk/government/uploads/system/uploads/attachment_data/file/609971/Clerking_competency_framework.pdf

ISCG, *Manual for Governing Bodies and their Clerks*, 15th edn, 2015

Governors Virtual Office, www.schoolleadershipsystems.com, on-line tool to manage the governing board's work and communications

GovernorHub, www.governorhub.com, on-line tool to manage the governing board's work and communications

There are five providers of the Governance Clerking Development programme. A list is on www.gov.uk/government/publications/licensees-professional-development-for-school-governors

Complaints

DfE, *Best Practice Advice for School Complaints Procedures 2016*, departmental advice, www.gov.uk

Countering terrorism and radicalism

DfE, *The Prevent Duty*, departmental advice, www.gov.uk

CEPA, *Security, Safeguarding and the Curriculum*, cepa.hope.ac.uk/media/liverpoolhope/contentassets/documents/media,83105,en.pdf

Curriculum

The Schools and Education section of the DfE's part of www.gov.uk gives details of the curriculum for both maintained schools and academies, including the National Curriculum

DfE, *Promoting Fundamental British Values as Part of SMSC in Schools*, departmental advice, www.gov.uk

Data

Analyse School Performance. An explanatory video is on YouTube, www.youtube.com/watch?v=A7sFQiEQdMY&feature=youtu.be. Access to each school's report is through the DfE's "Secure Access" portal, https://sa.education.gov.uk/idp/Authn/UserPassword

DfE. A tool for comparing data between schools is provided by the DfE on www.compare-school-performance.service.gov.uk

ESFA, *Understanding Your Data: A guide for school governors and academy trustees*, https://assets.publishing.service.gov.uk/government/uploads/system/uploads/attachment_data/file/721362/Understanding_your_data_a_guide_for_school_governors_and_academy_trustees.pdf

Fischer Family Trust, *School Dashboard*, for each subscribing school on www.fftaspire.org. The Fisher Family Trust also provides an e-learning module on using its dashboard, ASP and the Ofsted Inspection Data Summary Report, https://elearning.fft.org.uk

Data protection

DfE, *Data Protection: Toolkit for schools*, helps schools develop policies and processes for managing data in line with GDPR, on https://assets.publishing.service.gov.uk/government/uploads/system/uploads/attachment_data/file/702325/GDPR_Toolkit_for_Schools__1_.pdf.

Information Commissioner's Office, *Guide to the General Data Protection Regulation (GDPR)*, https://ico.org.uk/for-organisations/guide-to-the-general-data-protection-regulation-gdpr

Drugs

DfE, *DfE and ACPO Drug Advice for Schools*, 2012, www.gov.uk

Educational research bodies

The Education Policy Institute is an independent research institute that aims to promote high quality education outcomes for all children and young people, https://epi.org.uk/publications-and-research/

Institute for Education, a faculty of University College London, conducts research on all aspects of education, internationally as well as nationally, www.ucl.ac.uk/ioe/about

National Foundation for Education Research (NFER) is an independent educational research and assessment development organisation, www.nfer.ac.uk/research

Sutton Trust commissions research to influence policy and inform programmes that can improve social mobility through education

Equality

Guidance on equality in public sector organisations is given by the Equality and Human Rights Commission, www.equalityhumanrights.com, under Advice and Guidance>Public Sector Equality Duty

Exclusions

DfE, *Exclusion from Maintained Schools, Academies and Pupil Referral Units in England: Statutory guidance*, www.gov.uk/government/publications/school-exclusion

Federation

School Governance (Federations) (England) Regulations 2012 and *The School Governance (Constitution and Federations) (England) (Amendment) Regulations 2016*, www.legislation.gov.uk

NCTL, *The Governance of Federations*, www.gov.uk

Female genital mutilation

DfE, *Multi-Agency Statutory Guide on Female Genital Mutilation*, www.gov.uk

Finance

The DfE publishes various financial advice documents under "School Resource Management" on www.gov.uk, including a procurement guide *Buying for Schools* (www.gov.uk/guidance/buying-for-schools), a planning checklist, a guide to workforce planning, a benchmarking checklist and *Schools Financial Value Standard and Assurance*, a guide to completing the forms, www.gov.uk/guidance/schools-financial-value-standard-and-assurance-sfvs. Go to www.gov.uk/government/collections/schools-financial-health-and-efficiency.

Guidance from the Education Funding and Skills Agency on academy funding and the use of financial resources, including the *Academies Financial Handbook*, is on www.gov.uk under "Academies: funding, payments and compliance"

Free schools

New Schools Network, www.newschoolsnetwork.org

Freedom of information

The Information Commissioner's Office, www.ico.org.uk. Guidance and clarification on the application of the Freedom of Information Act

Governing board improvement

David Marriott, *Challenge: How governors can challenge school leaders effectively*, Adamson Publishing, 2017

Ofsted, *School Governance: Learning from the best*, 2011 and *Improving Governance: Governance arrangements in complex and challenging circumstances*, 2016

Various documents are on the Guidance Centre pages of the NGA's website, under "Improving your governing board", www.nga.org.uk.

Governing board self-review

All Party Parliamentary Group on Education, Governance and Leadership, *Twenty Questions Every Governing Board Should Ask Itself* and *Twenty-One Questions for Multi-Academy Trusts* (see pages 78–81), www.nga.org.uk

DfE, *A Competency Framework for Governance: The knowledge, skills and behaviours needed for effective governance in maintained schools, academies and multi-academy trusts*, www.gov.uk/government/publications/governance-handbook

"External reviews of governance" and "External reviews of governance: what's involved"(NCTL) on www.gov.uk give an overview of the external review process. The latter links to *External Review of Governance – Tool for facilitated self-review*, a template for self-review built on the four core areas recommended for use by external reviewers.

EES for Schools, *Governance Self Evaluation Tracker (GSET)*, www.eesforschools.org/targettracker

GLM Partnership, *Governor Mark*, www.glmpartnership.org

Governorline
Free helpline for governors, on 0800 151 2410 between 09:00 and 20:00 Monday to Friday (excluding bank holidays). Questions can also be emailed to governorline@entrust-ed.co.uk.

Institute of Chartered Secretaries and Administrators, *Academy School Governance Maturity Matrix*, www.icsa.org.uk

Wellcome Trust and NGA, *A Framework for Governance*, www.nga.org

Governing board succession

National Co-ordinators of Governor Services, *Succession Breeds Success: How to grow leaders in your governing board*, www.ncogs.org.uk

Governor on-line training

Modern Governor, part of The Learning Pool, a training and support organisation, has a suite of online training modules for governors, www.moderngovernor.com

NGA Learning Link is a suite of online training modules for governors and clerks to governing boards, www.nga.org.uk

Headteachers/principals and governors

DfE, *The School Governance (Roles, Procedures and Allowances) (England) Regulations 2013*, www.legislation.gov.uk/uksi/2013/1624/contents/made

DfE, *The School Governance (Roles, Procedures and Allowances) (England) Regulations 2013: Departmental advice*, www.gov.uk

DfE & NGA, *Recruiting a Headteacher*, www.gov.uk/government/publications/recruiting-a-headteacher

NGA, NAHT, ASCL and LGA, *What Governing Boards Should Expect from School Leaders and What School Leaders Should Expect from Governing Boards*, available to members on the NGA website, www.nga.org.uk

Martin Pounce, *Headteachers and Governing Bodies: a practical guide to making the partnership work*, Adamson Publishing, 4th edn, 2016

Health and safety

DfE, *Health and Safety: Advice for schools*, www.gov.uk

Health issues

DfE, *School Food in England*, www.gov.uk – departmental advice on the food to be provided in schools

The School Food Plan, www.schoolfoodplan.com – organisation with practical advice to improve take-up of healthy school food

See also MENTAL HEALTH

Inspection

Ofsted, *School Inspection Handbook*, www.gov.uk

Ofsted, *Common Inspection Framework: Education, skills and early years*, www.gov.uk

Insurance
Academies Risk Protection Arrangement (RPA), www.gov.uk. An alternative to insurance for academies, where losses that arise are covered by UK government funds

Learning outside the classroom
The Council for Learning Outside the Classroom has a variety of resources, www.lotc.org.uk

Looked-after children
Various documents can be found on the DfE section of www.gov.uk under "Looked-after children", www.gov.uk/topic/schools-colleges-childrens-services/looked-after-children

Mental health (children's)
Mentally Healthy Schools, www.mentallyhealthyschools.org.uk, contains practical resources to improve awareness, knowledge and confidence in promoting and supporting pupils' mental health

DfE, *Supporting Mental Health in Schools and Colleges*, 2017

GL Assessment, *Children's Well-being: Pupil attitudes to self and school*, 2018

National Children's Bureau, *A Whole School Framework for Emotional Well Being and Mental Health: A self-assessment and improvement tool for school leaders*, 2016

NSPCC, *Supporting Children with Mental Health Issues*, 2017

New governors
Start Here: A guide for new governors, Adamson Publishing, 8th edn 2016

NGA, *Welcome to Governance*

Parent governors
Joan Sallis, *Parent Governors: Your own guide*, Adamson Publishing, 2012

Parents
NGA, *Knowing Your School: Engaging parents*, www.nga.org.uk

Information and guidance on many aspects of parenting, including school admissions and becoming a governor, are on www.gov.uk

Parent View, section of the Ofsted website where parents can answer a 12-question survey ascertaining their views of their child's school, http://parentview.ofsted.gov.uk

Parentkind, www.parentkind.org.uk, organisation supporting parent participation in schools. Previously PTA UK.

PE and Sport Premium
Youth Sport Trust, *A Guide for Governors: Maximising the impact of the primary PE and sport funding*, www.youthsporttrust.org

The Youth Sport Trust website also provides good practice examples of

the use of the premium
Case studies of successful use by schools are given by the DfE under
"Improving school sport and measuring progress", www.gov.uk

Performance management
See APPRAISAL

Policies
DfE, *Statutory Policies for Schools*, www.gov.uk

Prevent duty
See COUNTERING TERRORISM AND RADICALISM

Procurement
DfE, *Buying for Schools*, gives advice on getting value for money and on
procurement law, www.gov.uk/guidance/buying-for-schools
DfE, *Schools Financial Efficiency: effective procurement*, video with
practical buying tips to achieve best value
Information specifically for governors is given by the DfE under "Schools
Financial Efficiency: Top ten planning checks for governors" on
www.gov.uk

Pupil behaviour
Various documents, including *Behaviour and Discipline in Schools:
Guidance for governing bodies*, can be found in the DfE section of
www.gov.uk

Pupil Premium
The DfE has various documents on the Pupil Premium on www.gov.uk,
including *Evaluation of Pupil Premium, Pupil Premium: funding and
accountability for schools, Pupil Premium Reviews* and *The Pupil
Premium: analysis and challenge tools for schools*
NFER/DfE, *Supporting the Attainment of Disadvantaged Pupils:
Articulating success and good practice*, www.nfer.ac.uk/publications/
pupp01
NGA, *Pupil Premium: Assessing the impact guidance*, www.nga.org.uk
Education Endowment Foundation/Sutton Trust, *Teaching and Learning
Toolkit*, guides schools on how to use their resources to improve the
attainment of disadvantaged pupils, https://educationendowment
foundation.org.uk. Its Families of Schools database enables you to
compare how Pupil Premium children in your school perform in
comparison with those in similar schools.
Teaching Schools Council, *Guide to Effective Pupil Premium Reviews*,
www.tscouncil.org.uk/wp-content/uploads/2016/12/PPR-guide-Spring-
2016-refresh-FINAL-1.pdf

Pupil voice
Children's Commissioner for England, www.childrenscommissioner.gov.uk
School Councils UK, www.schoolcouncils.org

Recruitment of governors

Academy Ambassadors, www.academyambassadors.org, helps find senior people from business and the professions willing to join MAT boards

Governors for Schools (previously SGOSS), www.governorsforschools. org.uk, supplies a free search and selection service for governing boards wanting to recruit candidates with commercial experience

Inspiring Governance, www.inspiringgovernance.org, connects skilled volunteers interested in serving as governors and trustees with schools and colleges

Recruitment of staff

See APPOINTING AND RECRUITING STAFF

Religious education

DfE, *Religious Education in English Schools*, non-statutory guidance, 2010, www.gov.uk

Safeguarding

Disclosure and Barring Service, www.gov.uk/government/organisations/ disclosure-and-barring-service

DfE, *Keeping Children Safe in Education*, statutory guidance, www.gov.uk

Educate Against Hate, website giving parents, teachers and school leaders practical advice on protecting children from extremism and radicalisation, www.educateagainsthate.com

Ofsted, *Inspecting Safeguarding in Early Years, Education and Skills from September 2015* contains a checklist, intended for inspectors but also useful for governors assessing their safeguarding arrangements

UK Council for Child Internet Safety (UKCCIS) *Online Safety in Schools and Colleges: Questions from the governing board* lists questions on child internet safety for governors to ask their school managements, www.gov.uk/government/groups/uk-council-for-child-internet-safety-ukccis

See also CHILD PROTECTION

School details

Get Information about Schools, www.gov.uk/guidance/get-information-about-schools. Database of educational establishments across England and Wales, maintained by the DfE

Schoolsnet, www.schoolsnet.com. Lists schools throughout the UK, giving a profile of each

School self-evaluation

Ofsted, *School Inspection Handbook*, www.gov.uk

Self evaluation by governing board

See GOVERNING BOARD SELF-REVIEW

Special Educational Needs and Disability

The DfE section of www.gov.uk contains a range of documents,

including the *SEND Code of Practice: 0 to 25 years* and *Schools: guide to the 0 to 25 SEND code of practice*
NASEN (National Association of Special Educational Needs), www.nasen.org.uk, has guidance on SEND for its members. NASEN also runs the SEND Gateway, www.sendgateway.org.uk/about.html, a free online portal providing links to a wide range of information, resources and training for those supporting children with SEND.

Staffing
DfE, *Staffing and employment: advice for schools*, www.gov.uk/government/publications/staffing-and-employment-advice-for-schools
NGA, *Knowing Your School: Finance and staffing*, www.nga.org.uk
See also APPRAISAL and TEACHERS' PAY

Teachers' pay
DfE, *Implementing Your School's Approach to Pay: Guidance for maintained schools and local authorities*, www.gov.uk
DfE, *School Workforce Planning: Guidance for schools*, www.gov.uk/government/uploads/system/uploads/attachment_data/file/584465/School_workforce_planning_guidance.pdf
School Teachers' Pay and Conditions Document, on the DfE website, www.gov.uk

Teacher Workload
DfE, *Reducing Teacher Workload*, www.gov.uk/government/publications/reducing-teachers-workload/reducing-teachers-workload
DfE, *Teacher Workload: Poster and pamphlet*, www.gov.uk/government/publications/teacher-workload-poster-and-pamphlet
DfE, *Workload Reduction Toolkit*, www.gov.uk/government/collections/workload-reduction-toolkit

Training for governors
Contact your local authority or consultancy, and see GOVERNOR ON-LINE TRAINING
See also CHAIRING and CLERKS.

Who's who in education

Secretary of State for Education	Damian Hinds
Minister, schools	Nick Gibb
Under Secretary, children & families	Nadhim Sahawi
Under Secretary, school system (incl. governance)	Lord Agnew
Shadow Secretary of State for Education	Angela Rayner
HM Chief Inspector of Schools	Amanda Spielman
National Schools Commissioner	Dominic Herrington (interim)

The names are correct at the time of going to press but can change any time.

The governing board

Maintained schools

Size: The governing board must have a minimum of seven members. There is no maximum.

Parents: There must be a minimum of two elected parent governors. The governing board may choose to have more elected parent governors, or may co-opt some parents as governors (but these will be co-opted governors not parent governors).

Headteacher: The headteacher has a right to a place on the governing board. He or she may waive that right, but the place remains open to them at any time if they later change their mind.

Staff: One governor must be a staff governor elected by the staff. The staff governor can be a teacher or a member of the support staff.

Local authority governor: There is one place for a governor appointed by the local authority. The governing board may detail and publish specific skills that it requires of such a governor before an appointment is made. If it does not consider that the person nominated by the local authority meets the eligibility criteria, it can refuse to appoint the person.

Members of staff cannot be appointed as LA governors.

Co-opted governors: The governing board can appoint as many of these as it wishes. Some may be members of the school's staff (in addition to the elected staff governor), but the total of staff members – including the staff governor and the headteacher – is limited to a maximum of one third of the governing board.

Foundation and partnership governors: In foundation and voluntary schools the proportion of foundation/partnership governors is protected. Voluntary controlled schools and foundation schools that do not have a foundation must have a minimum of two partnership/foundation governors, but the total number must not exceed a quarter of the governing board. In foundation schools with a foundation that are not trust schools ("qualifying foundation schools") the foundation governors must number at least two and not make up more than 45% of the entire governing board. In trust schools and voluntary aided schools the total number of foundation governors should outnumber all the other governors by two.

Associate members: Governing boards may appoint associate members, to sit on committees.

Skills: All appointed governors should, in the opinion of the appointing body, have the skills required to contribute to the effective governance and success of the school. The appointing body is:

- the governing board in the case of local authority governors and

parent governors who are appointed because it is not possible to fill the places by election
- the foundation in the case of foundation governors
- the relevant religious body for partnership governors of schools with a religious character
- the governing board for partnership governors of schools without a religious character.

Note that this requirement applies to local authority governors even if the governing board has not published the specific skills it requires.

Term of office: Between one and four years. The governing board can appoint individuals or categories of governors to different lengths of office.

Removal: The governing board can remove any governors that it has appointed and any elected governors, i.e. parents or staff, where there are serious or persistent issues with their conduct.

Chairs: The governing board can elect joint chairs if it considers this to be appropriate.

Academies

The DfE publishes model Articles of Association which new academies and free schools are expected to use. Some of the provisions have changed over the years – for example, it was only compulsory to have one elected parent governor before 2010. The DfE revised its model Articles at the end of 2017 and encourages schools with older versions to revise their Articles in accordance with the new models. The following is based on the current models, and will not necessarily apply in detail to older academies.

There are three levels of governance: members, who appoint the trustees and are roughly akin to shareholders of companies; trustees, who administer the academy, similar in function to directors of a company; and optional local governors, who have such powers in individual schools as are delegated to them by the trust.

There must be a minimum of three trustees, with no upper limit. There must be two trustees elected by the parents (see below on multi-academy trusts). The other trustees are either appointed by the members or by the foundation/sponsor, or may be co-opted by the trust. No more than one third of the trustees may be employees of the academy; this includes any teachers who are co-opted as trustees. It is common, but not compulsory, for the members to appoint the principal/chief executive as a trustee, if he or she agrees.

The term of office of a trustee is four years.

The *Academies Financial Handbook* recommends that larger trusts meet more than three times a year, and where a trust meets less than six times a year it must explain in its governance statement how it maintains adequate oversight of the budget.

"Local authority associated people" (such as LA employees or councillors) may not represent 20% or more of the membership of the trust. Their appointment must be authorised by the LA.

In multi-academy trusts (MATs) the trust may establish a local governing body or academy committee for each school in the trust; a local governing body can govern more than one school. The powers delegated to this body will be determined by the trust. In general, the trust sets the ethos and the general strategic direction of the school, while the governing body oversees the day-to-day management and operation of the school, but this is not universal. If each local governing body has two elected parents on it, there is no obligation to have parents on the trust board.

Committees

The governing board of a maintained school can have whatever committees it wants, or none. They commonly divide into those handling finance, the curriculum, staff and pupils, but premises, Special Educational Needs, extended services and other subjects may be handled by separate committees or be included in the terms of reference of others.

The trust of an academy also has a free hand in appointing committees. A local governing board or advisory committee will also be a committee of the trust, so if it in turn delegates responsibilities on finance, staffing etc, it will be to a sub-committee.

Either two or three governors must be appointed to conduct the headteacher's appraisal in a maintained school. They have to be supported by an external adviser. Academies may elect to follow the same procedure.

Governing boards of maintained schools should also set up pay committees, usually of three individuals, to deal with the headteacher's pay and monitor pay decisions for other staff.

Maintained schools may appoint non-governors as associate members to serve on committees, with voting rights. They may attend the full governing board meetings if the governing board so decides, but cannot vote.

Appeals and exclusions panels

There should be governors in readiness to hear staff appeals, judge parental complaints, consider pupil exclusions and, if relevant, hear admissions appeals.

A member of staff given notice of dismissal, unhappy with the decision on their pay or refused a promotion across the threshold, has the right to appeal to a panel of governors. Likewise, in certain conditions, parents have a right to appeal to a panel of governors about exclusions, complaints or admission decisions. A governing board may elect fixed panels each year to deal with these, but this is not obligatory and if it decides not to it is advisable to establish lists of governors from which to draw members to deal with them if and when required. When formed, each panel should have three or five members, and be clerked by an independent clerk.

Compliance with statutory requirements

The following list is based on one that was originally produced by Ofsted for inclusion in the school's self-evaluation form. It has been updated to reflect current requirements.

The curriculum

1. Every learner receives the **full statutory curriculum** that the school must provide.

2. The school provides teaching of **religious education** for all learners in accordance with the locally agreed syllabus (or otherwise, in accordance with relevant prescribed exceptions) and has told parents/carers of the right to withdraw their children.

3. The school provides a daily act of **collective worship** for all learners and has told parents/carers of the right to withdraw their children and, where applicable, has also told sixth formers of their own right to withdraw.

4. The school has a written policy on **sex and relationships education**, and has made it available to parents/carers.

5. *(Schools with pupils of primary age)* The governing board has decided whether or not to provide sex and relationships education (other than that required by the National Curriculum) and, if doing so, has agreed the content and organisation of the programme and has told parents/carers about it and about their right to withdraw their children.

6. *(Schools with pupils of secondary age)* The governing board has agreed the content and organisation of its programme of sex and relationships education and has told parents/carers about it and the right to withdraw their children (other than from what is required by the National Curriculum).

7. The school meets fully the learning and development requirements of the **Early Years Foundation Stage** (if applicable).

Equality & diversity

8. Under the terms of the Equality Act 2010 and subsequent regulations, governing boards are required to draw up **equality objectives** every four years and annually publish information demonstrating how they are meeting the aims of the general public sector equality duty. (See pp. 32–5.)

Learners with learning difficulties and/or disabilities

9. The school meets its requirements in Part 3 of the Children and Families Act 2014 and has regard to the **Special Educational Needs and Disability Code of Practice** when meeting learners' special educational needs, publishes its policy and makes it known to parents/carers and reports annually on the success of its policy.

10. The school meets the requirements of Part 4 of the Disability Discrimination Act 1995 (DDA) and any subsequent requirements and has regard to the Disability Rights Commission code of practice for schools (2002). The school informs parents/carers of its accessibility plan and **disability equality** scheme and reports annually on progress made on them.

11. The school has appointed a **special educational needs coordinator** and has ensured that the post holder has received training.

Learners' care and well-being

12. The school has procedures in place to ensure it meets all relevant **health and safety** legislation.

13. The school has a **child protection policy** and procedures in place that are in accordance with local authority guidance and DfE guidance and locally agreed inter-agency procedures (and the policy is made available to parents/carers on request).

14. Where the governing board provides **school lunches** and/or other school food, it ensures that they meet current DfE standards (this does not apply to some academies). Infant and primary schools must provide free meals for children in Reception and Years 1 and 2.

15. If applicable, the school complies with the welfare requirements of the **Early Years Foundation Stage.**

16. If relevant, the school must supply independent **careers** advice for pupils in years 9–13. (Applies to academies through their Funding Agreements.)

17. The governing board must ensure that the school makes arrangements to support children with **medical conditions.**

Informing parents/carers

18. The headteacher and/or governing board as appropriate ensures that all statutory **assessments** are conducted and results are forwarded to parents/carers and appropriate bodies.

19. The headteacher ensures that each year a **report on each learner's educational achievements** is forwarded to their parents/carers (only compulsory in a maintained school).

20. The school keeps **parents/carers and prospective parents/carers informed** by publishing information on SATS or GCSE results, admission arrangements, the school's ethos and values, the most recent Ofsted report, the charging and behaviour policies, information on the school's curriculum, and details of how the school meets the needs of children with SEND. This information must either be published on the school's website, or the website must indicate where it can be found.

21. The school publishes information on the amount of **Pupil Premium** the school has received for the current academic year, details of how it is intended that the allocation will be spent, details of how the previous academic year's allocation was spent, and the effect of this expenditure on the educational attainment of the relevant pupils.

22. A primary school must publish on its website details of how it spends

its **PE and sport premium,** including information on its impact on pupils' PE and sport participation and attainment.

Leadership and management

23. The governing board of a maintained school completes the **Schools Financial Value Standard** and submits it to the local authority by 31 March each year.

24. The trust of an academy produces **annual audited accounts,** a financial statement, a directors' report and an accounts return, and publishes the accounts on its website by 31 January each year. Management accounts are produced monthly, are given to the chair and the most recent ones are examined by the trust board at each meeting.

25. The responsibilities of the governing board, its committees, the headteacher/principal and staff in respect of finances are clearly defined and limits of **delegated authority** are delineated.

26. The governing board of a maintained school has an **appraisal** policy and a **pay** policy and ensures that all teachers, including the headteacher, are appraised in accordance with statutory requirements.

27. The governing board of a maintained school has secured that the provisions in the *School Teachers' Pay and Conditions Document* and any associated regulations relating to terms and conditions, including appraisal and induction, have been implemented for all teachers and the headteacher.

28. The governing board has all relevant **complaints and appeals** procedures.

29. The school meets the current government requirements regarding **safeguarding children** and safer recruitment, including maintaining a central record of recruitment and vetting checks. The requirements include the Prevent Duty to protect children against being drawn into terrorism, and the obligation to report known cases of female genital mutilation.

30. The governing board ensures that **childcare** not provided directly by the school is registered, where this is required by the Childcare Act 2006, and complies with all necessary registration requirements.

31. The governing board/trust publishes a list of its governors (maintained schools) or trustees, members and local governors (academies) and details of the structure and responsibilities of the governing body/trust and its committees on the school's website, together with their register of interests, and sends details of its trustees/governors to the DfE portal Get Information about Schools.

Guidance on statutory policies and documents is also provided by the DfE on the Gov.uk website, www.gov.uk/government/publications/ statutory-policies-for-schools. See also the Compliance section of the Governance Handbook *for more detail on trustees' and governors' compliance responsibilities, and the* Academies Financial Handbook *for specifics of academies' reporting duties on finance.*

What governing boards must ensure schools publish

- The school's name, address, phone number and a contact name
- SATS results, with percentages of pupils reaching expected standards in KS2 tests and average progress in the SATs subjects *or* GCSE results, with Progress 8 and Attainment 8 scores, percentage of pupils achieving a good pass in English and maths and percentage achieving the EBacc
- where school performance tables can be accessed
- the school's admission arrangements and oversubscription criteria, or a link to them
- a statement of the school's ethos and values
- the most recent Ofsted report, or a link to it
- Pupil Premium information and information on Year 7 Literacy and Numeracy Catch-up Premium in secondary schools
- report on the use of the PE and Sport Premium (primary schools)
- information on the school's curriculum for each academic year, including GCSE and approved vocational courses at Key Stage 4, phonics or reading schemes used at Key Stage 1, and PSHE; plus how people can find out more about the school curriculum
- a report on how the school meets the needs of children with SEND, including admissions arrangements and the accessibility plan
- the school's equality objectives
- details of the school's behaviour policy
- the school's charging and remissions policy
- the school's complaints policy/procedure
- careers programme information
- a list of the governing board/trustees/members, a register of their interests, their term of office and who appointed them, a record of their attendance and the committee structure with names of chairs
- annual reports and accounts (academies).

The above must be on the school website. Also schools must:

- keep pupils' curricular and educational records and provide parents with access to them
- report at least annually to parents on their children's progress and educational achievements
- provide a report to school leavers
- make sure that the pupils' educational records and common transfer files (CTF) are transferred securely to schools to which pupils move.

A governing board/trust must also make available agendas, approved minutes and papers of its meetings and committees with delegated powers.

Statutory duties of local authorities

Local authorities still hold significant powers and responsibilities for schools. This is a summary of their relevant duties.

Place planning and admissions: Ensure that there are sufficient pupil places, at both primary and secondary level, to educate the children in their area, and give special regard to the placement of children with SEND. Act as the admissions authority for community and voluntary controlled (VC) schools (unless it has delegated these powers). Provide parents with a collated set of admission arrangements for schools in the area, and provide support and assistance to parents in making a preference. Restrict class sizes for pupils aged 4-7 in maintained schools to 30 per class (some exceptions permitted).

Funding: determine the budget share for schools and PRUs, and distribute funds, including the Pupil Premium, to maintained schools (until 2020). May suspend a maintained school's budget if it considers it necessary. Establish a schools forum and ensure people are elected to it. Ensure that maintained schools complete the Schools Financial Value Standard.

School staff: Check that teachers about to be appointed to maintained schools are qualified. Is the legal employer of staff in community and VC schools.

Looked after children: Promote the educational achievement of looked after children.

Early Years: Ensure early years services are available to all families. Collect data on children in EY provision and ensure it is accurate and consistent. Secure sufficient Children's Centres to meet need.

SEND: Bring together education, health and social care agencies to assess whether a child needs an EHC plan. Publish a local offer of the support available for children with SEND. Fund children with EHC plans.

Safeguarding: Investigate suspicions that a child may be suffering harm and decide whether to take action to safeguard or promote the child's welfare. Appoint a Designated Officer who coordinates child safeguarding issues. Establish a Local Safeguarding Children Board. A general duty to safeguard and promote the welfare of children "in need".

Health and Safety: ensure the health and safety of pupils, employees, and visitors to schools where it is the employer, including producing a policy that such schools must adopt (this duty has many ramifications).

Curriculum and Assessment: Ensure that the curriculum delivered by maintained schools is broad and balanced and meets statutory requirements. Collect teacher assessment information in Key Stage 1, quality assure it and submit it to the DfE. Visit a percentage of schools administering Key Stage 2 tests during the period of the tests to ensure they are being administered correctly. Monitor primary schools to ensure phonics screening check is being properly administered.

Religious Education: Establish a standing advisory body on religious education (SACRE). Ensure that maintained, foundation and voluntary schools in its area deliver appropriate religious education and provide daily acts of worship.

Standards: Intervention duties are spelled out in *Schools Causing Concern*; they include issuing warning notices, appointing additional governors or applying to the Secretary of State to replace the governing body with an interim executive board where a school has been put in an Ofsted category or has failed to comply with a warning notice.

Academisation: Facilitate conversion of a school for which the Secretary of State has issued an academy order.

Governance: Make the instrument of government for each maintained school and federation of maintained schools. Set up the temporary governing body of a new school. Ensure the provision of training and information appropriate to their role for school governors, free of charge to the individual governors. Nominate individuals for appointment by governing bodies as Local Authority governors. Make the necessary arrangements for the election of parent and staff governors for community and VC schools, or delegate to headteachers. Provide clarity to governing bodies about what can be charged for.

Pupil Referral Units (PRUs): Establish management committees of PRUs.

Excluded pupils: Provide education for pupils from the sixth day of a permanent exclusion, and arrange to provide education for children unable to attend school because of illness. Ensure funding follows an excluded pupil to their next educational provider. Establish independent review panels to hear appeals against exclusions from maintained schools.

Boarding pupils: Ensure that sufficient but not excessive fees are charged to parents to cover the cost of children boarding in maintained schools in its area.

Absent children: Identify, as far as possible, those children in its area absenting themselves from school; initiate the issue of Attendance Orders and fixed penalty notices; initiate prosecution proceedings for unauthorised absence.

Parent Governor Representatives (PGRs): Appoint PGRs to their Overview and Scrutiny committees, or to other committees with the same function.

Travel to school: Make provision for suitable home to school travel arrangements for eligible children of compulsory school age (5-16) to facilitate attendance at a relevant educational establishment.

School estates: Maintain the buildings and premises in schools for which it is responsible in such a condition as does not put pupils or others at risk. Develop accessibility strategies to facilitate better access to education for disabled pupils.

Term dates: Establish term dates for maintained schools.

Role of Regional School Commissioners

According to the DfE, the main responsibilities of Regional School Commissioners (RSCs) include:

- taking action where academies and free schools are underperforming
- intervening in academies where governance is inadequate
- deciding on applications from local authority maintained schools to convert to academy status
- improving underperforming maintained schools by providing them with support from a strong sponsor
- encouraging and deciding on applications from sponsors to operate in a region
- taking action to improve poorly performing sponsors
- advising on proposals for new free schools
- advising on whether to cancel, defer or enter into funding agreements with free school projects
- deciding on applications to make significant changes to academies and free schools.

Currently they also have a role in intervening in maintained schools. Those judged to be coasting have to submit their improvement plans to their local RSC, who then decides whether these plans are adequate or whether to initiate academy conversion. RSCs may also issue warning notices to maintained schools that are causing concern. However, the Secretary of State announced in May 2018 that these powers are under review and that only an Ofsted judgement of inadequate will lead to forced academisation.

RSCs can also decide on changes to an academy's admissions arrangements and on applications from non-faith academies to be exempt from the requirement to provide a religious education that is broadly Christian in character.

The regions covered by each RSC are eight in number:

East of England and North-East London; East Midlands and the Humber; Lancashire and West Yorkshire; North of England; North-West London and South-Central England; South-East England and South London; South-West England; West Midlands.

For further information see "About Us" on the School Commissioners Group page of Gov.uk (www.gov.uk/government/organisations/schools-commissioners-group/about).

Governing board self-evaluation

The following sets of questions have been drawn up by the All Party Parliamentary Group on Governance with the National Governance Association to help school governing boards assess themselves.

Twenty questions every governing board should ask itself

Governing board effectiveness

Right skills: Do we have the right skills on the governing board?

1. Have we completed a skills audit which informs the governor specification we use as the basis of governor appointment and interview?

Effectiveness: Are we as effective as we could be?

2. How well do we understand our roles and responsibilities, including what it means to be strategic?

3. Do we have a professional clerk who provides legal advice and oversees the governing board's induction and development needs?

4. Is the size, composition and committee structure of our governing board conducive to effective working?

5. How do we make use of good practice from across the country?

Role of the chair: Does our chair show strong and effective leadership?

6. Do we carry out a regular 360° review of the chair's performance and elect the chair each year?

7. Do we engage in good succession planning so that no governor serves for longer than two terms of office and the chair is replaced at least every six years?

8. Does the chair carry out an annual review of each governor's contribution to the governing board's performance?

Vision, ethos and strategy

Strategy: Does the school have a clear vision and strategic priorities?

9. Does our vision look forward three to five years, and does it include what the children who have left the school will have achieved?

10. Have we agreed a strategy with priorities for achieving our vision with key performance indicators against which we can regularly monitor and review the strategy?

11. How effectively does our strategic planning cycle drive the governing board's activities and agenda setting?

Engagement: Are we properly engaged with our school community, the wider school sector and the outside world?

12. How well do we listen to, understand and respond to our pupils, parents and staff?

13. How do we make regular reports on the work of the governing board to our parents and local community?

14. What benefit does the school draw from collaboration with other schools and other sectors, locally and nationally?

Effective accountability

Accountability of the executive: Do we hold the school leaders to account?

15. How well do we understand the school's performance data (including in-year progress tracking data) so we can properly hold school leaders to account?

16. Do governors regularly visit the school to get to know it and monitor the implementation of the school strategy?

17. How well does our policy review schedule work and how do we ensure compliance?

18. Do we know how effective performance management of all staff is within the school?

19. Are our financial management systems robust so we can ensure best value for money?

Impact: Are we having an impact on outcomes for pupils?

20. How much has the school improved over the last three years, and what has the governing board's contribution been to this?

Twenty-one questions for multi-academy trusts

Vision, ethos and strategy

1. Does the Trustee Board have a clear vision and strategic priorities for the next three to five years, to which all academies contribute and which is understood by each of its academies?

2. How effectively do these strategic priorities drive the governance structure, activities and agenda setting at all levels of the Trust?

3. What vision does the Trustee Board have for the size of the Trust and how does the strategy ensure that there is the capacity to support any additional academies well?

Governance structures

4. Is the structure of the Trust from its members to academy level governance conducive to effective working, ensuring checks and balances but avoiding duplication at different levels, and delivering good two-way communications?

5. How does the Trustee Board ensure that its governance structure is clear, in keeping with its Articles of Association, and that those at regional, cluster and academy level understand their roles and responsibilities compared to those of the Trustee Board?

6. a) Does the Trustee Board have a scheme of delegation, is it published on its website and those of its academies, and does the scheme make clear where the following key governance functions are exercised:

determining each individual academy's vision, ethos and strategic direction?

recruiting each academy's Principal/Head of school?

performance management of each academy's Principal/Head of school?

determination of Human Resources policy and practice?

oversight of each academy's budget?

assessment of the risks for each academy?

b) Is the principle of earned autonomy applied to individual academies or local clusters and if so, do all involved at all levels of governance within the MAT understand how?

Trustee Board effectiveness and conduct

7. Right skills: Has the Trustee Board adopted a robust and transparent process for the recruitment both of trustees and those at local governance level, including role specifications, skills audits and interview panel to ensure those carrying out governance functions have the full range of experience, qualities and skills necessary to discharge all the Trustee Board's responsibilities?

8. Clerking: Does the Trustee Board have a professional clerk providing information and guidance on regulatory practice and procedures, including governance leadership to the committees and any academy level governance?

9. Chair: How does the Trustee Board ensure the chair shows strong and effective leadership?

10. Trustee performance: Does the chair carry out an annual review of each trustee's contribution to the Board's performance and ensure each trustee is investing in his/her own development?

11. Succession planning: Do we engage in good succession planning so that, in normal circumstances, no trustee serves for longer than two terms of office and the chair is replaced at least every six years?

12. Conflicts of interest and conduct: How does the Trustee Board ensure conflicts are avoided and that the Nolan principles of public life [https://www.gov.uk/government/publications/the-7-principles-of-public-life] are adhered to?

13. Learning from others: Has the Trustee Board regularly reviewed its structures and practice, making use of other Boards' experiences and periodically seeking external expertise?

Engagement

14. How does the Trustee Board listen to, understand and respond to pupils, parents, staff and local communities across all its academies?

15. What benefit do the academies within the Trust draw from collaboration with other schools and other sectors, including employers, locally and nationally; and how is the Trust involved in contributing to improving leadership and schools beyond its own academies?

Effective accountability of the executive leadership

16. How well does the Trustee Board understand its academies' performance data, and how do Trustees know that pupils in all their academies are making the best progress they can?

17. What mechanisms does the Trustee Board use to ensure there is a strong and effective executive leadership structure and personnel in place across the Trust with the right skills, clear line-management and reporting mechanisms?

18. How does the Trustee Board ensure senior leaders within academies are challenged to improve the education of pupils, and what intervention would be used if improvement is not progressing according to plan at an academy?

19. How does the Trustee Board ensure that the Trust's financial capability and management systems are robust to ensure compliance with the *Academies Financial Handbook*, best value for money and deliver the long-term strategy?

20. Do the compliance systems give assurance to the Trustee Board that the Trust is meeting its statutory and legal responsibilities?

Impact on outcomes for pupils

21. How much have the academies improved over the last three years, and what has the Trustee Board's contribution been to this?

With thanks to the National Governance Association and the All Party Parliamentary Group on Education, Governance and Leadership
© 2015 APPG & NGA

The National Curriculum

Subjects are divided into core and other foundation. The core subjects are compulsory for all pupils in maintained schools.

Core subjects
English, mathematics and science (and Welsh in Wales)

Other foundation subjects
Computing, PE – compulsory at all key stages

Art and design, design and technology, geography, history, music – compulsory at KS1–3

Foreign languages – compulsory at KS2 and KS3 (must be a modern language at KS3; see also note on EBacc below)

Citizenship – compulsory at KS3–4

In KS4 students have a statutory entitlement to be able to study a subject in each of four entitlement areas: the arts (art and design, music, dance, drama and media arts), design and technology, the humanities (geography and history) and modern foreign languages.

Religious education is not a core subject but is compulsory.

PSHE is not compulsory, but schools must make provision for it and are required to promote the spiritual, moral, social and cultural development of pupils.

Sex and relationships education is only compulsory at KS3 and 4. (However, relationships education is scheduled to become compulsory in primary schools in September 2019.)

Careers education and work-related learning are compulsory at KS4.

The English Baccalaureate

The following GCSE subjects constitute the English Baccalaureate (EBacc): English (both literature and language), maths, geography or history, the sciences (combined science or three individual sciences), a foreign language.

A pupil's average score is calculated by taking an average of the points they scored in the five EBacc subject areas. A point is the same as a grade in a new GCSEs (e.g. grade 8 is 8 points), while old style GCSE grades are translated into points using a DfE table. A school's EBacc average point score is calculated by adding together the EBacc average point score for all pupils at the end of key stage 4 and then dividing by the number of pupils in the group.

Attainment levels and floor standards

Primary schools

Pupils are tested in English reading, English grammar, punctuation and spelling (GPS) and mathematics in Key Stage 2 SATs. The tests produce a numerical score. To allow for differences in difficulty in the tests from year to year, the pupils' raw scores are then scaled. A scaled score of 100 represents the "national standard" and indicates that the pupil is at the desired level to start secondary school (pupils with scores below 100 are not held back).

A primary school is deemed to be below the floor standard if 65% or fewer of its pupils achieve the national standard in reading, GPS and mathematics at the end of KS2 and they have not made sufficient progress across all of the three subjects. "Sufficient progress" is calculated by comparing the KS2 results with those achieved at the end of KS1. Because KS1 tests will have used the old system of levels, the government has published a conversion table to give an equivalent to a scaled score.

A system of measuring children's starting point at Reception, so as to be able to assess progress, is being piloted in 2019–20 and will be introduced nationally in autumn 2020 (see page 55).

Secondary schools

Secondary schools are assessed according to Progress 8. Progress 8 records progress made by a pupil from the end of primary school to the end of secondary school. Each pupil's score is calculated by comparing their average grade across eight subjects with the average grade of all pupils nationally who started secondary school at a similar level.

The eight subjects are mathematics, English, three subjects from the English Baccalaureate, and three subjects that can be other GCSE qualifications (including those qualifying for the EBacc) or any other non-GCSE qualifications on the DfE approved list. English and maths are given double the weight of other subjects. Put together, their scores in the eight subjects are a pupil's "Attainment 8".

A secondary school is below the standard if:

- its Progress 8 score is below -0.5, and
- the upper band of the 95% confidence interval is below zero (i.e. allowing for the size and nature of the cohort.)

For more on Progress 8 see www.gov.uk/government/uploads/system/uploads/attachment_data/file/536052/Progress_8_school_performance_measure.pdf.

The floor standards and coasting measures are to be combined into a single measure in the near future.

Common terms, acronyms and abbreviations

APPG   *All Party Parliamentary Group; in the context of governance usually the APPG on Education, Governance and Leadership*

ARE   *Age-related expectation – the level of learning expected of a child at a given age*

ASCL   *Association of School and College Leaders*

ASP   *Analyse School Performance*

ATL   *Association of Teachers and Lecturers*

AWPA/U   *Age-Weighted Pupil Allocation/Unit – unit used to calculate a school's funding, weighted according to the pupils' ages.*

BME/BAME   *Black and minority ethnic*

BTEC   *Business and Technology Education Council – name also given to the qualifications it awards for vocational courses*

CAF   *Common Assessment Framework – a standardised approach to assessing and meeting a child's additional needs*

CAMHS   *Child and Adolescent Mental Health Services*

Cohort   *Body of pupils entering a school in any one year*

CPD   *Continuing Professional Development*

DBS   *Disclosure and Barring Service*

DfE   *Department for Education*

DO   *Designated officer, appointed by the local authority, to whom child protection cases involving allegations against school staff and volunteers must be referred*

EAL   *English as an Additional Language*

EBacc   *English Baccalaureate, which pupils are deemed to have achieved if they gain A*–C GCSEs in English, maths, geography or history, two sciences and a foreign language*

ESFA   *Education and Skills Funding Agency – body responsible for funding academies, Free Schools and 16-19 provision*

EHC plan   *Education and Health Care plan – support for children with pronounced Special Educational Needs*

Estyn   *Inspection body for education and training in Wales*

FE   *Further Education*

FGB   *Full governing board*

FGM	*Female genital mutilation*
FTE	*Full Time Equivalent – part-time staff measured according to how many full-time staff would be required to work the same number of hours*
GAG	*General Annual Grant – annual funding for an academy*
G&T	*Gifted and talented*
GDPR	*General Data Protection Regulations*
HE	*Higher Education*
HMCI	*Her Majesty's Chief Inspector – the head of Ofsted*
HMI	*Her Majesty's Inspector, an inspector employed by Ofsted*
ICT	*Information and Communications Technology*
IDSR	*Inspection Data Summary Report*
IEB	*Interim Executive Board – temporary board of governors appointed to replace an inadequate governing board*
IEP	*Individual Education Plan*
INSET	*In-Service Training for Teachers*
ISR	*Individual School Range – categorisation of a school according to size and type used in calculating the salary level of a headteacher*
KS1(2/3/4)	*Key Stage One (Two/Three/Four). The term Key Stage Five is sometimes used to describe the sixth form level.*
LA	*Local Authority*
LSA	*Learning Support Assistant*
MAT	*Multi-academy trust*
MLD	*Moderate Learning Difficulties*
NAHT	*National Association of Head Teachers*
NASEN	*National Association for Special Educational Needs*
NASUWT	*National Association of Schoolmasters/Union of Women Teachers*
NCOGS	*National Association for Coordinators of Governor Services – the representative body for managers of governor service departments*
NCTL	*National College for Teaching and Leadership*
NEET	*Not in education, employment or training*
NEU	*National Education Union*
NGA	*National Governance Association*
NLG	*National Leader of Governance – an experienced and skilled governor available to help governing boards*
NPQH	*National Professional Qualification for Headship*

NQT	*Newly Qualified Teacher*
NVQ	*National Vocational Qualification*
Ofqual	*Office of the Qualifications and Examinations Regulator*
Ofsted	*Office for Standards in Education, Children's Services and Skills*
PPA	*Preparation, planning and assessment time – designated non-teaching time for teachers*
PRU	*Pupil Referral Unit*
PSA	*Parent Support Adviser*
PSHE	*Personal, Social, Health and Economic education*
PTA	*Parent Teacher Association*
QTS	*Qualified Teacher Status*
RSC	*Regional School Commissioner*
SACRE	*Standing Advisory Council for Religious Education – body which advises on religious education and worship*
SATs	*Standard Assessment Tests – commonly used (though unofficial) name for National Curriculum tests. Also single academy trusts*
SD/IP	*School Development/Improvement Plan*
SEAL	*Social and Emotional Aspects of Learning*
SEN	*Special Educational Needs*
SENCO	*Special Educational Needs Co-ordinator*
SEND	*Special Educational Needs and Disabilities*
SFVS	*Schools Financial Value Standard*
SLT	*Senior Leadership Team*
SMSC	*Spiritual, moral, social and cultural*
STEM	*Science, technology, engineering and maths*
STRB	*School Teachers' Review Body – group that advises the government on teachers' pay and conditions each year*
TA	*Teaching assistant*
TLR	*Teaching and Learning Responsibility – management responsibility for which a teacher receives extra pay*
TRA	*Teaching Regulation Agency*
TUPE	*Transfer of Undertakings (Protection of Employment)*
UCAS	*Universities and Colleges Admissions Service*
UTC	*University Technical College*
VA	*Voluntary Aided*
VC	*Voluntary Controlled*

Useful organisations

For governors

National Governance Association (NGA)
The national membership organisation for governors in England.
36 Great Charles Street, Birmingham B3 3JY ☎ 0121 237 3780
governorhq@nga.org.uk www.nga.org.uk

Freedom and Autonomy for Schools – National Association (FASNA)
National forum for self-governing primary, secondary and special schools, academies and multi-academy trusts. George Spencer Academy, Arthur Mee Road, Stapleford, Nottingham NG9 7EW ☎ 0115 917 0142 c.robson-farrelly@fasna.org.uk www.fasna.org.uk

Governorline
A free helpline for governors and clerks of all state schools. Lines are open between 09:00 and 20:00 Monday to Friday except bank holidays, 0800 151 2410. *Or email* governorline@entrust-ed.co.uk.

Information for School and College Governors (ISCG)
Provides advice and runs seminars. PO Box 3934, Gerrards Cross SL9 1AG ☎ 07934 067402 iscg@governors.uk.com www.governors.uk.com

Inspiring Governance
Scheme run by Education and Employers with the NGA that recruits people from business and the professions interested in becoming governors and enables governing boards to contact them 22-4 Red Lion Court, London EC4A 3GB ☎ 020 7566 4880
info@educationandemployers.org www.inspiringgovernance.org

Governors for Schools (previously SGOSS)
Charity that recruits people interested in becoming school governors and passes details on to schools. c/o 2nd Floor, 29 Ludgate Hill, London EC4M 7JR ☎ 020 7354 9805 info@governorsforschools.org.uk www.governorsforschools.org.uk

Government and other national bodies

ACE Education 72 Durnsford Road, London N11 2EJ ☎ 020 888 3377 (business and training enquiries) advice line 0300 0115 142
enquiries@ace-ed.org.uk www.ace-ed.org.uk

Advisory, Conciliation and Arbitration Service (ACAS) online help service on website plus helpline: 0300 123 1100 www.acas.org.uk

Catholic Education Service 39 Ecclestone Square, London SW1V 1BX

☎ 020 7901 1900 email through Contact a Diocese on
www.cesew.org.uk

Church of England Education Division Church House, Great Smith
Street, London SW1P 3AZ ☎ 020 7898 1000 www.churchofengland.
org/more/education-and-schools. The Church advises contacting the local
diocesan education office with individual enquiries.

Department for Education (DfE) (enquiries) Ministerial and Public
Communications Division, DfE, Piccadilly Gate, Store Street, Manchester
M1 2WD ☎ 0370 000 2288 0370 To email use the online contact form
on www.gov.uk/government/organisations/department-for-education. The
DfE is also on Facebook, www.facebook.com/educationgovuk, Twitter
(@educationgovuk), and YouTube, www.youtube.com/user/
educationgovuk.

Disclosure and Barring Service (DBS) DBS Customer Services, PO Box
3961, Royal Wootton Bassett, SN4 4HF ☎ 03000 200 190
customerservices@dbs.gsi.gov.uk www.gov.uk/government/organisations/
disclosure-and-barring-service

Equality and Human Rights Commission (EHRC)
www.equalityhumanrights.com/en For advice go to The Equality
Advisory and Support Service (EASS), FREEPOST, EASS, HELPLINE,
FPN6521 ☎ 0808 800 0082 email through form on the website
www.equalityadvisoryservice.com.

Office for Standards in Education, Children's Services and Skills (Ofsted)
☎ 0300 123 1231 email contact form: https://contact.ofsted.gov.uk/
contact-form www.gov.uk/government/organisations/ofsted

Office of the Qualifications and Examinations Regulator (Ofqual)
Spring Place, Herald Avenue, Coventry CV5 6UB ☎ 0300 303 3344
public.enquiries@ofqual.gov.uk
www.gov.uk/government/organisations/ofqual

Office of the Schools Adjudicator osa.team@osa.gsi.gov.uk
www.gov.uk/government/organisations/office-of-the-schools-adjudicator

Welsh Government, Department for Education and Skills Cathays Park,
Cardiff CF10 3NQ ☎ 0300 060 4400 customerhelp@gov.wales
http://gov.wales/topics/educationandskills/?lang=en

Governance in Wales

Summary of the main differences from England

Legislation	National Assembly for Wales has full legislative powers on Education
Regulatory bodies	Separate bodies for Wales on Curriculum and Assessment, and Post-16 Education, part of Welsh Government. Separate General Teaching Council (still in operation)
Curriculum	New curriculum being developed for feedback in April 2019 Foundation Phase for 3- to 7-year-olds, based on experiential learning Extra compulsory subject up to KS4 (Welsh; English in Welsh-medium schools) Learning Pathways for 14- to 19-year-olds Welsh Baccalaureate for 16+, with a heavy skills base
Assessment and testing	Wales has kept the A*-G grades for GCSEs, and A2 continues to contribute to overall A Levels National tests for reading and numeracy supplement teacher assessment
League tables	Not in Wales, but schools are rated by government green, yellow, amber or red according to their effectiveness
School governance	Significant differences from England especially on composition of governing bodies, e.g. provision for two associate pupil governors from Y11, 12, or 13 to be nominated through school council. *(Governance constitution has been under review for some time.)* Mandatory training for new governors and chairs
"Reforms"	No specialist schools, trust schools, academies, or Free Schools Statutory requirement for schools to have development plans
Inspection	A different regime in Wales, including inspection body, Estyn
Finance	Education SSA is indicative only. LAs fix funding levels of schools
Teachers' pay	Wales bound by same statutory provision as England
Reporting to parents	Governors present an Annual Report to Parents. Parent bodies have the right to demand up to three meetings a year with governors.

Annual workplan

The planner on the next few pages consists of lists of the main governing board tasks, organised by term, together with some special tasks or events. The lists of tasks are divided into the three categories that cover most governing board activity: Resources (including finance, staffing and premises); Curriculum and Achievement (standards); Pupils, Families and the Community (including pupil welfare and communications).

Governing boards of maintained schools in England may delegate most of their decision-making powers either to committees or to individuals, within certain restraints (see *The School Governance (Roles, Procedures and Allowances) (England) Regulations 2013*). Those things that cannot be delegated to an individual, only to a committee, are the alteration or discontinuance of the school, a change of category of school, approval of the first formal budget plan of the financial year, the determination of admission arrangements or the admission of a particular child, the decision to appoint a new headteacher or deputy (though the appointment process must be delegated), the suspension of a governor, and the exclusion of pupils. On the other hand, governing boards must delegate to panels or committees the hearing of appeals on pupil discipline, staff dismissals and decisions on staff pay and promotion.

The powers of delegation of the governing board of an academy trust are specified in its Articles of Association, but it is usually stated that they are left to its own discretion. In MATs some or most of the powers may be delegated to local governing bodies/academy committees.

Where delegation is to an individual, in practice this will probably mean the headteacher/principal, or to one or two governors, possibly including the headteacher/principal.

The only items that have to be dealt with by the full governing board of a maintained school are those which relate to the constitution of the governing board itself, such as reconstitution, the election or removal of the chair or vice chair, co-option of governors, choice and terms of references of committees, length of terms of office, appointment of the clerk, and the appointment of a headteacher or deputy. The governing board may also decide whether to have associate members on committees and whether they can attend full governing board meetings.

In the following lists items in bold type are ones which *have* to be considered each year. For most of these, regulations do not state when they should be done, but we have placed them in what is generally regarded the best term for them. Some tasks can be performed at any particular time of the school year, and these are listed on the next page.

The DfE publishes both mandatory and advisory timelines for academies and maintained schools, on www.gov.uk. These can give updated information on tasks and on statutory requirements.

Items to be addressed at the first meeting of the year

Full governing board

Review the range of committees in place and their terms of reference. Elect members and appoint clerks to committees and either elect chairs or agree to delegate this to each committee. Review governor monitoring links

Appoint governors to specific responsibilities as required: training and links with LA governor services, safeguarding, Pupil Premium pupils, SEND

Review individual governors' curriculum/faculty/class/special area responsibilities

Discuss operating guidelines for the governing board, including governor visits

Set objectives of the governing board for the year, linked to SDP

Agree a programme of meetings for the year, including committees

Elect chair and vice chair (academy trust)

All committees

Elect chair (if not done by full governing board)

Examine School Development/Improvement Plan

Items that may be undertaken at any time

Elect chair and vice chair, if their term of office has expired (maintained schools usually at first meeting of year)

Consider and agree school's self-evaluation

Appoint clerk

Report on any racist incidents and the response, at least annually

Items that should be done on a regular basis

Monitor School Development Plan (all committees)

Review/write new policies. Draw up framework for policy review (all committees)

Reports on training attended by governors and discussion of training needed (full GB)

Receive reports:
> from the headteacher/principal (termly) (full GB)
> from committees (full GB)
> on governors' visits to the school (full GB)
> from the safeguarding governor (full GB or PFC com.)
> on parental complaints (without details) and outcomes (full GB or PFC com.)
> on incidents of bullying and racism, and the responses (full GB or PFC com.)
> from the governor/committee with responsibility for SEND (PFC com.)
> from individual governors and staff on their curriculum areas (C&A com.)
> from the designated teacher for looked-after children (PFC com.)

Review pupil progress and attainment (C&A com.)

Items that should be included on each agenda

Declaration of pecuniary interests

Receipt and consideration of apologies

Autumn term

For full governing board

If the school is an admissions authority (academies, foundation and VA schools) draw up admissions policy for the next school year

Initiate review of the School Development Plan

Receive and consider report on unvalidated data on pupil performance contained in the school's ASP report

Publish list of trustees and members (academies)/governing board members and associate members (maintained schools) on website

Update and publish register of pecuniary interests

Issue statement on use of Pupil Premium

Resources

Monitor budget

Appoint governor(s) for Health & Safety

Complete asset management plan

Conduct head's appraisal – advisable for an academy

Review and determine the head's salary (backdated to 1 September) – advisable for an academy

Receive report on teacher appraisal process and ensure that pay panel has made/confirmed pay decisions on all teachers

Curriculum and achievement

Review National Curriculum test, GCSE and other exam results

Set pupil performance targets

Pupils, families and the community

Receive annual report on safeguarding children

Review net capacity of the school

Plus items listed under "first meeting of year"

To note

September Final wave of new National Curriculum subjects to start being taught in secondary schools
New *Keeping Children Safe in Education* statutory guidance comes into force

October Admissions applications to secondary schools close (31st)

December Submit audited accounts and auditor's regularity assessment report to EFA by 31st (academies)

Spring term
For full governing board
Review implementation of School Development Plan (or divide task among committees)

Issue statement on use of PE and Sport Premium (primary schools)

Publish proposed admissions arrangements for autumn of the next year (schools that are admission authorities)

Agree budget for the new financial year (maintained schools) (may not have to be submitted until early in Summer term)

Resources
Review staff pay policy (maintained schools)

Review charging and letting policy (together with PFC com)

Draft budget for the coming year (maintained schools)

Review insurance (academies)

Review staff structure

Submit Schools Financial Value Standard (maintained schools)

Report on gender pay differences (academy trusts with over 250 staff)

Curriculum and achievement
Receive and discuss report on curriculum developments, especially in relation to teaching the National Curriculum

Review effectiveness of Pupil Premium funding

Pupils, families and the community
Revise prospectus information on the school's website (or in summer term)

Review charging and letting policy (together with R com)

Receive and discuss report on the working of the SEND policy

To note
January Admissions applications to primary schools close (15th)
Academies' audited accounts to be posted on website and sent to Charity Commission (31st)

February Local authorities confirm budgets for their maintained schools
EFA confirms academies' budgets (28th)
Admissions authorities to determine their entry arrangements (28th)

March National offer day for places at secondary schools (1st)
Schools Financial Value Standard (maintained schools) to be submitted to local authority by end of the month

Summer term
For full governing board
Conduct self-review of governing board effectiveness

Review implementation of School Development Plan (or divide task among committees)

Approve budget for coming school year (academies)

Resources
Audit school fund

Review appraisal policy (maintained schools – advisory for academies)

Review job descriptions

Review staff attendance

Appoint governors to conduct head's appraisal in the autumn, ensure they are or will be trained, and appoint external adviser

Curriculum and achievement
Review and monitor specified curriculum area

Pupils, families and the community
Report to parents on the SEND policy (not special schools)

Review child protection policy and procedures

Review attendance of pupils

Review pupil exclusions for the year

Receive report on progress in implementing accessibility plan

---

To note
April Start of financial year (maintained schools)

Updated information on meeting an objective under the Equalities Act to be published

National offer day for places at primary schools (16th)

May KS2 SATs week (14th–17th)

Last date (31st) for announcing any proposed redundancies from September

July Academy trusts to submit their budget forecast return (by end of month)

TIMING OF HEAD AND DEPUTY RESIGNATIONS
If they want to leave their jobs, headteachers have to hand in their resignations by 30 September, 31 January, 30 April for each term respectively and deputies by 31 October, 28 February, 31 May

Index